Studies and surveys
in comparative education

To Ambassador Barbara Newell
with kind regards
and looking forward to a
good cooperation

Charles Hummel

30.11.79

Education today
for the world of tomorrow

Charles Hummel

A study prepared for the

International Bureau of
Education

Published in 1977 by the
United Nations Educational,
Scientific and Cultural Organization,
7 Place de Fontenoy, 75700 Paris

Printed in Switzerland by Journal de Genève.

ISBN 92-3-101460-9
French ed.: 92-3-201460-2

Preface

The International Conference on Education, which is convened every two years by Unesco, is becoming increasingly important, inasmuch as it gives those responsible for education an opportunity to meet and discuss their common problems and to exchange experiences. The participation of a growing number of ministers and senior officials of the Member States of Unesco, as well as the volume and importance of the national reports prepared for this Conference, are enough to prove that it constitutes a genuine forum and meetingplace for those taking part in the effort to improve the education systems of the different countries.

After every session, the International Bureau of Education (IBE), as the Unesco organ responsible for holding the Conference, tries to present a picture of the world situation. For this purpose, it calls upon a specialist in the field and asks him to describe what seem to him to have been the developments, main trends and achievements in the field of education during the two preceding years. The resulting book is a personal work, but one which reflects Unesco's guiding principles and preoccupations, and is based on the educational policies and activities of its Member States. It is intended for a wider public than the Conference, in the hope that, thanks to an over-all perspective, teachers, parents and pupils will gain a better understanding of their own education system.

The author of this study, Dr. Charles Hummel, is eminently qualified for this task. First, in his capacity as Secretary-General of the Swiss National Commission for Unesco and also as that country's permanent delegate to Unesco, where he is also a member of the Executive Board, he has been collaborating with our Organization for years; as representative of Switzerland on the IBE's Council, he is particularly well informed about educational problems. These qualifications were recognized by the International Conference on Education when it appointed him Rapporteur General at its thirty-fifth session.

In introducing Mr. Hummel's book to the reader, I should like to express to him my own thanks and those of our Organization for his untiring efforts to promote international co-operation in the field of education.

AMADOU-MAHTAR M'BOW

Director-General,
Unesco.

Contents

Introduction

To try to summarize the main problems and trends of education in the world today is an undertaking which is at once both modest and ambitious. It is modest in so far as it is limited to a mere description of facts. After all, it is not my intention to defend any thesis or theory in this book. In these pages, I have tried to be as neutral an observer as possible and to outline the present situation and preoccupations of education. It is an attempt to describe what is happening, what are the problems and what is at stake—nothing more.

The point of departure of this book is the thirty-fifth session of the International Conference on Education (Geneva, 1975). That Conference examined major trends in education and devoted special attention to the following four topics: recent changes in policies in education and major educational problems; access to education, and more especially to higher education; innovation in education; lifelong education. The present work is pivoted around these topics. Is it necessary to stress the fact that the purpose of this undertaking is also an ambitious one—even too ambitious perhaps?

The limitations of this study are obvious. Some of them are determined by the movement which has affected the educational world as a whole. Anyone who tries to grasp its main lines at a given moment has little time for reflection and runs the risk of being overtaken by events. Other limitations are imposed by the necessary and rather arbitrary choice of sources of information, due, for example, to the fact that, among the major international languages, the author is unable to read either Arabic or Russian. The greater part of the information used here is derived from official sources. It therefore has a tendency to be over-optimistic. It may be that a reform or an innovation which is enthusiastically described by its promoters, and which appears worthy of interest, represents what is actually only a minor project.

One subject of paramount importance has not been tackled in these pages: the role and training of teachers. A parallel publication [1] is devoted to this question, which was a special topic at the thirty-fifth session of the International Conference on Education.

In this study, the present problems of education are divided into a number of chapters, each of which deals with a special topic. Fundamentally, however, each of these topics contains the whole. Each specific approach should enable one to develop all the problems raised in the field of education. The problem of education in rural areas, for example, is approached from the point of view of the relations between education and society. In this context, the 'ruralization of education' is a question which concerns both the more general one of development, and the relations between education and the world of labour. It is obvious, however, that the problem of the education of rural inhabitants could also be considered from the point of view of the democratization of education. For there is no doubt that one of the serious problems of education in rural areas is that of the inequality of teaching. In this field, as in others, rural inhabitants are clearly at a disadvantage as opposed to city dwellers. They are the ones who show the lowest rates of school attendance; they are the ones who have the greatest difficulty in obtaining access to higher education. However, an analysis of the problems of education in rural areas also leads directly to all the questions connected with lifelong education. In the country, all forms of out-of-school instruction, especially the education of adults and their relationship to the school, are playing an increasingly important role. The great majority of illiterates are to be found in the country. To a large extent, illiteracy is a rural problem.

Let us take another example: the question of participation. It is an essential aspect of any process of democratization. But the concept of lifelong education, as conceived at the present time, is based on the participation of all in the educational process taken as a whole. It goes without saying that the question of participation is a fundamental one as soon as we approach the subject of the relations between education and society.

1. Goble, N.M.; Porter, J.F. *The changing role of the teacher: international perspectives.* Paris/Geneva, Unesco; IBE, 1977. 234 p.

It is important to note that each of the major problems of education contains the sum-total of all the problems connected with the subject—as in one of Leibniz's monads. For this shows to what point educational problems constitute a whole. They form a system. If you touch one part of this system, you touch it all. In other words, every change in this system, every reform, every partial innovation, will have repercussions on the entire system. A measure taken at the nursery school level influences both the university sector and the relations between education and employment.

Anyone who tries to get an over-all view of education throughout the world has a natural tendency to generalize, to perceive similarities rather than differences, to see common problems rather than special preoccupations. However, while fully aware of the danger of over-simplification, one must admit that a very large number of questions arise in a similar way in socio-cultural contexts which are otherwise often very different. And there are many problems which are common to practically all countries, even if they show special features in each of them. (Incidentally, if that were not the case, comparative education would have little meaning, and any exchange of information in that field would be of little use.)

There are, obviously, certain major problems which apply only to a specific category of country. These are more especially the developing countries, which have to face enormous difficulties that are unknown in the industrialized countries. The situation of education in the Third World is often a tragic one because of the following characteristics which are peculiar to them: low rates of school attendance and consequently high rates of illiteracy; very high rates of grade repetition and educational wastage; education systems which are not adapted to the country's socio-cultural and economics needs (foreign systems inherited from the colonizers).

However, almost all countries are confronted with certain major tasks, such as the following: democratizing the education systems so that there will be greater equality not only in opportunities for access to different levels of education but also in opportunities for success in education; radically transforming the systems from the point of view of lifelong education, improving the effectiveness of teaching; creating closer links between school and society, between school and the working world, between school and cultural development; developing out-of-school education and especially adult education. It has already been emphasized that all these tasks are interdependent.

Moreover, they all have a political character, even if in part they appear in a 'technical' aspect.

Everywhere in the world we can find a growing awareness of the totality of problems. People are realizing more and more that the different sectors of education constitute a whole and that it is necessary to make the education system much more coherent in its entirety and at the same time—what is particularly important—to integrate it more closely in the broader social, economic, political and cultural context of the country. Accordingly, it would seem necessary, for example, to integrate educational policy with national policy or, more concretely, to plan education within the framework of a general development plan. Moreover, it might prove counterproductive to develop one part of the system without simultaneously developing the whole in an organic and harmonious way. The flight from the land or the unemployment of university graduates in some countries are examples caused by imbalances in the systems.

Education is one of the few great hopes of our time. In a ratioalistic world, it replaces a number of ancient myths and beliefs. It is through education that modern man believes a better future to be within his grasp. To educate is to mould the future.

There are many States—including some of the poorest—which are devoting one-fourth or even one-third of their national budget to education because they feel that education is an essential factor in their development.

Nearly half a century ago the visionary H.G. Wells wrote that a race had started between education and disaster.

This book would not have seen the light without the affection, constant encouragement and advice of my wife; without the initiative, friendly assistance and criticism of the staff of the IBE who have unceasingly helped me to compile the necessary information for this edition; and without the co-operation of various departments and officials of Unesco, and particularly its Office of Statistics.

Сн. H.

Aubais-Paris-Saxon
May–October 1976

Chapter One

Reforms
and innovations

Everywhere in the world, reforms and innovations are among the most urgent preoccupations of educational circles. They are one of the leitmotifs of any discussion today about educational problems. They are also an underlying theme in this book as a whole.

During the sixties, the 'world educational crisis' was a subject, in many countries, which stirred up discussions among circles interested in educational matters. In October 1967, an international conference was held on this topic at Williamsburg. Under this same title [26],[1] Philip H. Coombs published his critical analysis of the situation of education, which was specially prepared for that conference.[2] In some parts of the world, the famous 'May 68' and other similar phenomena were felt to be an explosion of this 'crisis of education'. Others saw in them the signs of a crisis of certain forms of society. But well before those spectacular events, many countries had already become aware of the problems raised by their education systems, which were suffering from a failure to adapt to a changing world. Major projects for educational reforms had already been launched or were in the planning stage. In some cases, particularly in Western Europe, the events of 1968 accelerated and accentuated the process of renovating the education systems. Since then, the educational world has entered into the change.

---

1. The figures in square brackets refer to bibliographical references at the end of the book.

2. A similar analysis to that given by COOMBS in *The world educational crisis* [26] is also contained in the report of the International Commission on the Development of Education established by Unesco: E. FAURE, et al. *Learning to be* [54].

The main directions of this movement are reflected in the different chapters of the present work: democratization, lifelong education, relations between education and society.

EDUCATIONAL REFORMS
AND THE GOALS AND OBJECTIVES OF EDUCATION

Every reform of an education system involves prior reflection on the goals of education, on its objectives, as well as on the role of educational institutions. In any innovation in this field, the desired educational objectives are modified, or at least questioned. Practically everywhere in the world of today, an awareness of the problems raised by education is intensifying this search for basic orientations or reorientations. This has been clearly shown by two recent meetings of groups of consultants on the 'philosophy and goals of education' organized by Unesco.[1]

Goals and objectives

The goals of education are the result of philosophical reflections on man, on human existence in its historical context and on the systems of relationships connecting man to nature and to the society in which he lives, creates and acts. The concept of a goal implies that man is a being launched towards a future which he hopes will be a better one. Are the ideals—such as truth, beauty, justice, liberty—which guide him in his effort to transcend his own condition and himself constant values and norms, in part at least? Or are they, in all cases, ideals whose very essence changes throughout ages and cultures? To what extent and in what conditions do new educational goals appear in the history of humanity? Do the mutations of societies of which we are witnesses engender new goals? As, for example, in relation to the search for a new international economic order? Only a systematic

---

1. The first was held in Geneva in June 1975; the second in Paris in June 1976 [113]. An extract of the conclusions of the first meeting was published in the review *Prospects* under the title: 'A hundred years ago, Nietzsche wrote...' [119p, p. 3-6]. Two of the communications presented were reproduced in the same periodical: Jean-Marie DOMENACH, 'Education and society in the context of the Western industrialized countries' [119p, p. 7-18]; and Bogdan SUCHODOLSKI, 'Education, between being and having' [119p, p. 163-80].

comparative analysis of the goals which determine the different education systems could provide answers to questions of this kind.

Contrary to goals, which always belong to the world of ideas and, while they indicate fundamental orientations, are never achieved, objectives fall within the domain of educational policy and are aimed at concrete solutions to the problems confronting societies. Every education system is characterized by the dialectical relationship existing between its goals and its objectives. Goals and objectives of education are emanations of value systems and norms which are also explicit in other cultural contexts: in myths and beliefs, in religions, philosophies, ideologies, literary works, etc. They correspond to the aspirations, structures and determining forces of the societies which have secreted them. They are characterized by three general indicators: the nature of man—the nature of society—the nature of knowledge [65, p. 3]. Every education system embodies a vision of man, a project of society and an ideal of knowledge.

An analysis of education systems reveals that they are based not only on explicit goals and objectives but also on implicit principles and orientations. The explicit goals and the implicit goals are far from coinciding at all times. The explicit goals and objectives are those expressed in constitutions, laws, official texts and declarations, political manifestos relating to the education system in question. But what are the real facts about these often grandiloquent declarations of intent? Practically all governments today affirm with conviction that in their countries education is based on respect for human rights, on equality, equity, non-discrimination, etc. But is there anywhere a truly democratic education system, free from all discrimination and in which equality of opportunities for success is guaranteed to all?

One example of this dichotomy of goals can be found in certain developing countries which denounce—and rightly so—the scandal of illiteracy, but which reserve the greater part of their educational funds for developing the secondary and university sector, while neglecting the primary sector of education, and more particularly adult literacy. Coming from all parts of the world, the participants in the Unesco meeting on 'educational goals and theories' noted on this subject that (in the Third World):

The choice of a foreign model was made by the ruling élite, with a view to perpetuating its own powers and privileges. This explains the curious fact that, in countries were there is an extremely high illiteracy rate, government spending on secondary and higher education has been much higher than on basic education. In the Third World, the education crisis is above all a crisis of goals [113, p. 6].

There are still many education systems whose implicit goals correspond to social norms of former times or to foreign cultures; this is the case with the majority of developing countries. Obviously, the search for really relevant goals and objectives should be carried out by taking account, on the one hand, of the present socio-cultural context and, on the other, of studies looking to the future. For all educational activity is essentially aimed at the future.

Towards new directions ?

Present reflections about the goals and objectives of education take account, or should take account, of a certain number of facts characterizing our time, such as the collapse of age-old systems of values; worldwide interdependence and the enormous inequities between societies and within some of them; the awareness of limited resources and global growth; the various anxieties about the possibilities of the destruction of mankind as a whole, of ecological disasters and famine; the demographic explosion; the whirlwind of change; more and more situations of conflict, etc.

Aurelio Peccei, the founder of the 'Club of Rome', has the following to say in his autobiography entitled *La qualité humaine:*

Man has moved from a defensive position, long subject to the imperatives of Nature, to a position of domination. He has acquired and is exercising the ability to influence everything on earth as he sees fit. Moreover, whether willingly or not, he ends up by directing his own future, but soon he will have to decide what road to follow. In other words, his new position of mastery forces him, in practice, to assume new regulatory functions which he will have to carry out, whether he wants to or not, in the face of those two closely connected systems Nature and mankind. ... The present global crisis, which is affecting the entire human system by creating within it all kinds of critical imbalances, is a direct consequence of the inability of the individual to rise to the level of understanding and responsibility which his new power requires of him. The problem is to be found in man himself, not outside him, and therefore any solutions will also have to be found within him. The primordial, essential thing is the quality of individuals [115, p. 51-2].

New goals of education are making their appearance.

Confronted with such a picture, the group which was considering the question of goals reached the conclusion that it was necessary for education to concern itself about the following values:

1. *Autonomy.* Give individuals and groups the maximum awareness, knowledge and ability so that they can manage their personal and collective life to the greatest possible extent.
2. *Equity.* Enable all citizens to participate in cultural and economic life by offering them an equal basic education.
3. *Survival.* Permit every nation to transmit and enrich its cultural heritage over the generations, but also guide education towards mutual understanding and towards what has become a worldwide realization of a common destiny [119p, p. 5].

Discourses on education often have a tendency to forget the child. After a certain time, however, we find that there is a rediscovery of the child and, consequently, an increased awareness of his specific needs. One proof of this is the growing interest in pre-school education and in the education of handicapped children.

Three examples

Everywhere, to some extent, people are now reflecting on the objectives of education. By way of illustration, we shall describe three results of this kind of study taken from very different sources.

In 1974, the New Zealand Ministry of Education published a report on the goals and objectives of education. In the heart of this document there is the following definition of education: 'Education involves those activities which extend the individual's ability to learn, relate, choose, create, communicate, challenge and respond to challenge so that he may live with purpose in the community of today and tomorrow and achieve satisfaction in the process' [46, p. 11]. This definition is based on the following eight basic principles:

> ...the search for meaning, purpose and identity in life is necessary for the health of both the individual and the community; every individual has a right to develop his abilities and a need to be accepted as a person; the community needs the participation and involvement of its members, who have individually and collectively a responsibility to contribute to their mutual development; every individual faces the task of reconciling conflicts between personal and community claims; every person has a right to enjoy being in community and so develop his capacity for living; learning to live

and work in community is a lifelong process in which every person is to some extent both teacher and learner; the development of skills and knowledge, and the development of social, ethical, and aesthetic attitudes and values are complementary processes; the diversity of cultures in New Zealand's heritage enriches the whole of our multi-racial society, which in turn should meet the needs of all ethnic groups and foster a sense of identity for each [46, p. 10-11].

The basic principles of public instruction in the USSR [1] are inspired by the ideal of a 'new man'—the man of a classless and truly democratic society, a man who is highly educated and cultivated, a true humanist who struggles for the happiness of all peoples of the world, a true internationalist who loves his people and at the same time respects other peoples. These principles are expressed in the following way: equal rights to education for every citizen of the USSR regardless of his race or nationality, his sex, his religion, his social status; compulsory education for all children and all young people; the governmental and public character of all educational institutions; freedom to choose the language in which one is taught; free education; an integrated system of public education and continuity in all types of educational institutions to ensure the possibility of transferring from a lower to a higher level of education; uniformity of communist instruction and education; co-operation between school, family and community in bringing up children and young people; liaison between education and practice in constructing a communist society; a high scientific level of education; the humanist and ethical character of education; co-education of persons of both sexes; the secular character of education.

Professor D.V. Ermolenko summarized the fundamental objectives of the education system in the USSR as follows: pre-school establishments, working in close co-operation with the family, should begin to educate and bring up children in a complete and harmonious way; they should protect and improve their health, instil in children elementary practical habits and a love of work, look after their aesthetic education, prepare them for school, bring up children with a spirit of respect towards their elders and with a love of the fatherland.

The goal of generalized secondary education in the USSR is to provide children and young people with an education in keeping with

---

1. This whole next passage is based on the statement made by Professor D.V. Ermolenko before Unesco's working group on the philosophy and goals of education in June 1976.

the present needs of social, scientific and technological progress, to instil in the pupils a healthy and profound knowledge of the fundamentals of the sciences, to develop in them a desire to keep on improving their knowledge and the ability to add to it themselves and use it for practical purposes. The school is called upon to develop in the younger generation a scientific attitude, an international and patriotic spirit, high moral qualities; it must promote a complete and harmonious development of the pupils and their cultural level, build up their health, perfect their aesthetic education, prepare them for work and social activities, as well as for the carefully considered choice of an occupation.... In modern conditions, when man's store of knowledge is tending to increase very rapidly, it is no longer possible to assimilate what is merely a certain number of facts. It is important to accustom young people to extend their knowledge of their own accord and to make their way through the floods of scientific and political information. Much still remains to be done in this field.

At the beginning of 1976, a Conference of Ministers of Education of the African Member States of Unesco was held at Lagos. In a Declaration, that Conference defined the 'aims, role and purpose of the educational process' as follows:

The far-reaching changes, not to say radical transformations, which must be introduced into existing educational systems are becoming an urgent necessity. They stem from the new mission which those responsible for education in Africa intend to assign to education in order to strengthen their independence, to make good the deficiencies caused by colonialism and to promote an authentic, modern African society. In this innovative context which, in many cases, is revolutionary in character, education should not only be made responsible for passing on values and knowledge to the younger generations, but should also produce fully conscious citizens and future productive workers in a dynamic context; it should alter ways of thinking and attitudes among individuals and among groups in order to initiate the necessary social changes and to provide an impetus to change in the direction of progress, justice and liberty.

The tasks

In this context, the main tasks of education are:

(i) to educate the young while at the same time awakening in them a critical awareness of the status of their peoples and developing in each individual the values of work, progress, and the cultural values of their civilization;

(ii) to inculcate and strengthen patriotism and dedication to all causes which are in the national interest;

(iii) to promote the spirit of mutual understanding and readiness to fight for the ideals of peace and universal solidarity;

(iv) to dispense general scientific and technical knowledge so as to secure the advancement of the nation and to underpin the all-round development of society;

(v)   to provide a new form of education so as to establish close ties between the school and work; such an education, based on work and with work in mind, should break down the barriers of prejudice which exist between manual and intellectual work, between theory and practice, and between town and countryside.

Practical objectives

In terms of practical objectives, all these tasks make it incumbent on African schools:

(i)   to share in the work of raising the intellectual level of the whole of society and, to this end, to penetrate society wherever needed so as to be accessible to every individual regardless of sex, age, social or economic status or of the milieu from which the individual comes. This objective makes it necessary for education to use national languages as the vehicle of thought and of science and technology;

(ii) to contribute to the economic development of the country by producing the necessary quantity of cadres of appropriate quality needed by the nation; ...

(v)   to democratize the structures as well as the content of education and to enable every individual who so requires and possesses the necessary potential to continue his vocational and cultural education in appropriate institutions and in appropriate forms;

(vi) to establish suitable links between education, training and employment activities, maintaining very close liaison with the environment or the local community as all-round development demands [21k].

These three approaches are very different, but in part more complementary than contradictory; it would be easy to add to them a long list of other attempts to clarify the goals and objectives of education. In connexion with goals, there would figure all the great ideals and aspirations of humanity: respect for human rights, peace, development, the 'quality of life', justice, etc. In analysing recent trends in the field of education, a certain number of objectives stand out, not all of which are perhaps really new but which, nevertheless, seem to be characteristics of our time. They will take on shape as we approach the various topics in this study; at this stage it is sufficient to mention some of the more significant ones. Above all, they relate to learning: learning to become someone; to create; to look after one's own education; to educate and to be educated; to work alone and in a group; to make choices between masses of information; to assume responsibilities; to communicate; to participate in the development of the community and in taking economic decisions; to respect differences in others; etc. Likewise, they relate to the development of certain abilities and attitudes, such as, for example, the development of language skills and self-expression, critical attitudes, the faculty of self-evaluation, etc. And lastly, they also include one objective which is almost universally recognized: that of permitting the free and full flowering of the personality.

The question of the goals of school instruction in a modern education system, a subject closely connected with that of objectives, will be dealt with later and in another context (see p. 51-3). However, one remark is called for at this time. There is a tendency to expect that the school (and education in general) can meet all challenges, remedy all calamities. As soon as a problem becomes too pressing or threatening—from pollution to drugs and sexuality, from mass media to politics, from development to peace—it is customary to invent a new educational programme. There is thus a danger that education may become the 'catch-all' of society, its alibi and conscience. It is the optimism of the Age of Enlightenment which persists in triumphing in this way.

When defining educational goals and objectives, we should be aware of the limitations of education.

Reforms

There is an impressive list of States which, beginning in the seventies, have instituted sweeping reforms of their education systems or enacted new laws governing the entire field of education: Algeria, Argentina, Benin, Costa Rica, Finland, the Federal Republic of Germany, Indonesia, Japan, Mexico, Pakistan, Peru, Spain, Sri Lanka, Togo, the United Republic of Cameroon, USSR, Uruguay, Yugoslavia. Important reforms are being prepared in Denmark, France, the Netherlands, Romania and Sierra Leone. Sweden has undertaken to carry out a permanent process of reform.

At the beginning of 1976, Colombia instituted an important and ambitious educational reform which was part of a general policy of social advancement and integrated rural development. It is aimed, on the one hand, at reducing the existing differences between the city and the country, between rich and poor, and, on the other, at accelerating the process of development. In the first place, basic primary education (five school years) will become universal, compulsory and free of charge. It will be followed by four years of basic secondary education. It is from this basic education that the Colombian Government expects the greatest return, the strongest influence on the country's development. The other sectors of education, from the pre-school to the university level, will also be developed, special emphasis being placed on a modern renovation of technical and vocational training, as well as on great flexibility in the system as a whole. Quantitative expansion will be backed up by an effort at qualitative improvement, especially by improved teacher training and by the use of new technologies. The administration of the system will be decentralized and will make it possible for the population to participate in educational matters.

Algeria is also engaged in carrying out a major reform of its education system, which, beginning in 1974, should be completed in 1985. The main lines of this reform are the following: on the structural level, the educational reform provides for a fundamental basic school, calling for nine years of compulsory attendance and providing a general polytechnical education, which means an education based on all the disciplines, and particularly on the sciences and technology, with a strong component of practical, productive and social work projects. Attached to this basic school, which constitutes the cornerstone of the new system, are institutions of general secondary education, or of shorter or longer vocational training. According to those responsible for this reform, the structures proposed by it are based 'on a permanent conception. Accordingly, none of the proposed channels constitutes an impasse or obstacle to individual advancement.' The system provides that not only school students but also other members of the public will have access to studies [1, p. 12-13].

A very daring reform is under way in the Netherlands. In 1975, the Ministry of Education and Sciences published a voluminous document: *Contours of a future education system in the Netherlands* [94], which gave rise to wide discussion throughout the country. These proposals provide for an extremely flexible and open education system, with easy transitions from one level to another, with opportunities for a 'second chance', with a system permitting young people who have left school to continue their studies while working full or part time, with a considerable development of adult education and the establishment of an 'open school' offering everybody a broad range of opportunities for self-education and training.

This plan provides for compulsory education for children from 4 to 16 years of age. This basic education would be followed by a 'high school' organized according to sectors of social activities: social services, science and technology, commerce, economics and administration, agriculture, communications, art. The over-all plan aims primarily at integrating and establishing the school and the whole education system as solidly as possible in the realities of society. Added to this picture of a progressive system is the fact that it provides for a high degree of political and administrative decentralization and the active participation in educational affairs of all the groups and classes concerned, but it will undoubtedly be a long time before it becomes a reality—twenty to twenty-five years, according to its authors.

Notwithstanding the examples we have just cited, one has the impression that the enthusiasm for major reforms has slowed down somewhat in very recent years. Among the probable causes of this trend, there are three which can easily be identified: (*a*) certain reforms have given disappointing results; (*b*) the economic crisis is stabilizing or reducing the budgets of ministries of education, which automatically puts a stop to expensive reforms; and (*c*) the shock of 1968 is fading away. There are also many reforms which bog down because the governments which planned them do not remain in power until they are completely implemented. After all, every reform depends on political will.

STRATEGIES OF INNOVATION

Although the impulse towards major reforms seems to be slackening, interest in innovations remains steady and is even increasing.

The practice of innovation in the field of education has always existed, of course, as there is no development or progress unless there is change, and there is no change without innovation. However, the idea of 'innovation in education' is a relatively recent one, as is also the thought being given to the significance and mechanisms of innovation in the field of education. 'I cannot remember that I ever heard the word "innovation" being used in educational contexts until six or seven years ago', wrote Torsten Husén [119e, p. 13].

What is the meaning of innovation in education ?

According to the Organisation for Economic Co-operation and Development's (OECD) definition, innovation is 'a deliberate attempt to improve practice in relation to certain desired objectives'. The OECD text adds that this definition 'does not exclude innovations which are also concerned with the shaping of new objectives or policies or functions unrelated to old objectives' [108d, p. 11].

Since innovation is always a creative act aimed at a future which should be an improvement over an unsatisfactory present, it therefore implies a vision of the future, the vision of a new man in a changed environment, and likewise a project of society. In every innovation, therefore, there must be a certain reorientation of the educational programme, in other words, genuine innovation always presupposes new objectives arising out of a search for the future. In every innovation, the very purpose of education is at stake.

Innovation is not a good thing in itself. It is only useful in so far as it is a driving force for progress. Innovation for innovation's sake, hasty and ill-considered innovation, on the other hand, can only disturb the educational processes. Innovation, therefore, should be based on serious research and experience. Innovation, and especially information about other people's innovations, may shorten the time needed for one's own research. However, it is only very seldom that innovations can be transferred in their original form from one country to another.

Opposition

Every innovation has to overcome opposition. Education systems are rightly charged with their lack of flexibility. They have the inertia of large administrative establishments and adapt themselves to change only with enormous difficulty. However, opposition to innovations is not exclusively internal. Besides the administrators, and especially the teachers, whose status and role—and routine—are almost challenged by an innovation, it is primarily the parents and the political parties who are opposed to change: the political parties because every reorientation in education has a political significance; the parents, because the ambitions which they cherish for their children are almost always based on traditional models.

One must never lose sight of the role played in the formulation of educational policies by the dreams and aspirations which parents have for their children. It is practically impossible to carry out an important educational reform against the will of the parents. Mark Blaug sees in this one of the reasons why the 'ruralization' of education in the developing countries has, up to now, always ended in failure [10, p. 51]. This is the risk which is likewise inherent in movements aimed at creating 'endogenous' education systems. They might also be considered as attempts to establish cut-rate education.

In this connexion, there is a revealing passage in the final report of the Meeting of Senior Officials of Ministries of Education of the Twenty-five Least Developed Countries, which was held in Paris, at Unesco, in September 1975:

> ... that the constraints in implementing the above changes and reforms are serious, that sudden political decisions in this field should be avoided and that the role of international co-operation in helping countries to overcome such constraints is relatively limited. This is particularly true in the area of traditional value systems and attitudes towards practical programmes and work; parents as well as teachers and teacher trainers are sometimes reluctant to accept non-academic orientations. The incentive systems in some of the LDCs are also hardly conducive to drastic changes in this respect: towns are often more attractive to the young than rural areas, academic degrees are thought more valuable for economic and social mobility than vocational training [86b, p. 6].

However, opposition to innovations and radical reforms is presumably greater in countries where school education already has a long tradition behind it. For this reason, the developing countries have particularly interesting models and solutions to offer for the education of tomorrow. Thanks often to international co-operation, in other words, thanks to the advice of the best specialists in the world, these countries can also show very modern education systems, drawing largely on the most advanced technologies. It seems likely that, in the very near future, the education systems of some developing countries will be in the van of educational progress. Moreover, it seems likely that a highly centralized education system is more resistant to innovations than a decentralized system. As Jean Hassenforder rightly observed:

> It is by innovation that a society gropes its way towards the future. In this way, innovation guides and enriches forward-looking thinking. Success or failure are not solely dependent on innovation, but also on its adaptability to the social realities of the time. A close relationship with the local environment is therefore necessary. Decentralized governments favour such a relationship [63, p. 115-16].

In view of the opposition which can frustrate even the most timely projects for innovation, the implementation of an educational reform has to be planned very carefully. Real strategies of innovation have been worked out in recent years. In these strategies, what matters is not to avoid conflicts but to settle them, for every educational innovation inevitably gives rise to conflicts.

A study of these extremely complex mechanisms of innovation can bring out a certain number of especially important points.

An educational reform should always be integrated in an over-all development policy of the State in question. (In this sense, all countries are in the process of development.) Only too often there is a tendency to forget that education is a sub-system of a socio-cultural system. The crises of education are very frequently the consequence of the fact that an education system which has been secreted by a society at a specific stage in its development persists without any major changes, while the society in question has undergone a transformation. There is therefore no longer any agreement between that society's system of values and the goals of its education system. In principle, the problem is the same in the case of an education system which has been received or imported from abroad, as has happened in the majority of the countries of the Third World.

An educational reform does not achieve its purpose unless it is in agreement with the general policy of the country. For example, a reform aimed at the democratization of education has no chance of success under an authoritarian régime. Likewise, an attempt to stop a flight from the land by educational measures cannot succeed unless there is also a policy in other sectors aimed at improving the condition of the farmers, as, for example, by taking steps to facilitate capital loans to agricultural co-operatives.

But policies also have to be in agreement within the education system itself. Innovations cannot succeed if they are contrary to the basic conceptions or main lines of development of the system as a whole. There would be no sense, for example, in trying to individualize education at the secondary level while trying to maintain rigid structures in the tertiary sector, i.e. if universities were supposed to remain just as they had been conceived in the nineteenth century.

When carrying out an innovation, it is necessary to realize that it can never continue to be an isolated action. Either it will be a failure, or it will have repercussions on the system as a whole and lead to other innovations.

The process of innovation is particularly complex because it takes place at several levels. A reform in education is generally decided on by a political authority (it is, in any case, a political act) and, in many cases, by a central body—but it does not become a reality until it reaches the classroom. For this reason, the implementation of an innovation in education is connected with all the problems concerning the centralization or decentralization of political power.

Many examples go to show that an educational innovation does not really succeed unless there is genuine participation by all those concerned. It involves a dynamic and dialectical process which calls for an uninterrupted dialogue with the 'users'. A reform or innovation cannot succeed against the wishes of the parents, the opinions of influential groups and persons, or the will of the teachers and pupils. The participation of the groups concerned presupposes adequate information. The mass information media (press, radio, television) have an important role to play and a great responsibility to assume during this period of maturing, which will be all the longer if the project is an ambitious one. However, information should be exchanged also through more direct contacts between those responsible for the innovation and their 'customers', for example, by meetings of parents and pupils. A community where an innovation is undertaken—such as the establishment of a community education centre—should have the feeling that it is its own project. In this connexion, the following remark, contained in the OECD study already quoted, appears particularly relevant:

> As we have observed throughout our analysis, the major problem is not that information does not exist, but rather that very few are interested and take energy to look for relevant information. The creation of a need for relevant information is probably more important than the expansion of the information service. This need is directly connected with the role the individual plays in the process. Only through real participation in decision making, in a dialogue with those concerned, and in active involvement in the development and evaluation stages, is it possible to create conditions for communication. An active partner is necessary if communication is to have any meaning [108d, p. 263].

In every renovating process in education, the co-operation of the teachers is essential, but it is also particularly difficult to obtain.[1]

---

1. 'The attitude of the teaching profession is what ultimately determines the success or failure of an innovation', says Jean THOMAS in his book, *World problems in education: a brief analytical survey* [143, p. 127].

On the one hand, educational innovation often acts as a challenge to the authority of the teacher in question, on the other hand, it makes retraining necessary. The teacher must therefore change his habits and his routine, possibly enter into new relations with his pupils, and in addition to these discouraging factors, he himself has to undergo a new training process. Continuing teacher training is therefore a prerequisite for the development and constant renewal of education systems.

However, continuing teacher training does not seem to be enough to ensure the active co-operation of the teaching staff in a process of far-reaching innovations. They must be integrated still more closely. This can be done at the research level. Since, in any case, every innovation should rest on solid and sufficiently well-tested scientific foundations, the participation in this research of those who are confronted with pedogogical problems every day is, however one may look at it, necessary in order to ensure that innovation projects will be practical and realistic.

In some countries, special structures have been created to assist the process of innovation. Sometimes they are merely information centres, in others they may be institutes of educational research, or even more complex bodies which not only define the objectives and practical details of a reform but also play a decisive role in carrying them out. Examples of such structures are the National Council for Innovation in Education in Norway, the Schools Council in the United Kingdom, the National Council of Education in Sweden, the National Council of Educational Research and Training in India, etc. However different these institutions may be in their actual organization, they all have one characteristic in common: 'They represent a necessary link between the formulation of a normative change at the policy level and the implementation of this policy' [108d, p. 101].

International co-operation

Although the problem of reforming an education system and that of educational innovations are essentially matters of national concern, it has recently been found that an important dimension is being added to them by regional and international co-operation.

With regard to educational innovations, the Organization for Economic Co-operation and Development (OECD) has done pioneer work by creating, in 1968, the Centre for Educational Research and Innovation (CERI). The purpose of this centre is to encourage and assist pilot experiments in the member countries of the OECD. Several projects have been planned around one promising innovation: the use of computers in higher education. In 1973, CERI published a work in four volumes containing case studies and a summary: *Case studies of educational innovation.* Vol. IV: *Strategies for innovation in education* [108d].

In an entirely different region, Asia, there is a programme of co-operation designed to encourage innovations in education which deserves to be described in somewhat greater detail: the Asian Programme of Educational Innovation for Development (APEID).[1] Its originality and principal characteristics are to be found in the fact that it is a network of national bodies, while the central institution which inspires and co-ordinates the programme as a whole is a regional body, the Asian Centre of Educational Innovation for Development (ACEID), established in Bangkok as an integral part of Unesco's Regional Office for Education in Asia. This programme was drawn up by the Regional Conference of Ministers of Education of Asia in 1971. At the present time, seventeen Asian States are participating in it. All of them have set up national groups for development with regard to educational innovations. The network is made up of these groups and the information and research centres. The participating States meet regularly to evaluate the programme as a whole, to define its future lines and to adopt concrete action projects.

The APEID is aimed at stimulating and encouraging educational innovation connected with problems of development in Asia. All the activities and projects which make up this programme must be planned, perfected and carried out jointly by the Member States. The fact that APEID is a regional programme means that the projects and activities which constitute it can be used and adapted in several countries of the region. The programme comprises six sectors: (*a*) new directions and structures in education; (*b*) educational administration; (*c*) the preparation of school programmes; (*d*) educational technology; (*e*) new structures and methods of teacher training; (*f*) science teaching.

The activities carried out in this connexion comprise, among others: an information service based on the case study; a visit and exchange programme; the organization of seminars and training courses for the staff of the associated centres; the creation of a network

1. See the article 'Asian Programme of Educational Innovation for Development (APEID): an example of a regional strategy', in *Prospects* [119k, p. 535-40].

of specialists capable of furnishing technical and advisory services to APEID and its Member States, particularly in the field of planning.

APEID's major objects of concern at the present time are: functional basic education for young people and adults; the development of education in rural areas; practical training; instruction in health and nutrition.

Examples of similar regional structures are to be found in other parts of the world. One example is the Council for Cultural Co-operation (CCC), established under the Council of Europe. In the near future, Unesco's programme envisages the creation of regional networks in Africa, the Arab States and Latin America.

A Commission for Drawing up a Strategy for Renovating Education in the Arab Countries was set up at the recommendation of the fourth Meeting of Ministers of Education of the Arab States, held at Sana'a in December 1972. A preliminary report has already been presented by this commission at the third session of the General Conference of ALECSO (Arab League Educational, Cultural and Scientific Organization), which was held at Cairo in January 1974. The final report was to be published by the beginning of 1977. All of this commissions's work of documentation, studies and reflection is based on the conviction that an Arab educational revolution is inevitable. This educational revolution finds its support in—and at the same time tries to strengthen—the factors of unity among the various Arab countries, and especially the community of language, culture and history which constitutes the very foundation of Arab identity. This search for identity, on which the desire for a renovation of education systems is based, is part of a general trend characterizing the development of ideas concerning education in most of the countries of the Third World.

In all these regional programmes concerning educational innovation, there is an important information component. However, the flow of documentation and information cannot be limited to one part of the world, and with this in mind Unesco set up an International Educational Reporting Service (IERS) in 1974 at the International Bureau of Education (IBE). This service became operational in 1975 and has already demonstrated the needs and opportunities for exchanges between educators of various countries. Every two months, the IBE publishes a bulletin, *Innovation*, containing articles and information on current experiments, and, also bimonthly, an *Awareness list* prepared from a computer printout which informs documentation, information and research centres about recent documents describing projects of innovation, or analysing the process of change itself. More detailed case studies are published in a series of booklets, *Experiments and innovations in education*, comprising more than twenty titles issued during the two years 1975-76. Lastly, the IBE tries to supplement this system with an 'Answer service' designed to provide direct information to institutions in need of documentation about questions relating to innovation and experimentation.

Chapter Two

Lifelong education: theory and practice

Lifelong education has existed ever since there have been men on earth who grow, who reflect, who are shaped by the vicissitudes of their lives, who acquire knowledge, experience and practical know-how. Lifelong education is a new conception of the educational process which is revolutionizing all the education systems of the world. This statement is only superficially paradoxical. Although it has always existed in practice, its conceptualization and a realization of the consequences which have to be drawn from it are only recent. The same thing has been true of other phenomena—electricity, the atom, chemical reactions, economic laws, psychological or social structures, etc.—which have changed the world only through their actual discovery, scientific analysis and the fact that advantage has been taken of the opportunities they offered for exploitation for the benefit of humanity.

The development of the concept of lifelong education, which can be compared with the Copernican revolution, is one of the most striking events in the history of education.

THE DEVELOPMENT OF THE CONCEPT

At all times, education has been a process which has not been limited with respect to either time or space. Everywhere, education has always been going on throughout life: in the family, in the clan, through initiation rites, the church, the school, in corporations, in work, in war, in the street, in the market, in every human relationship, in conversation, when listening to stories, myths and legends, readings books and newspapers, visiting museums, looking at the frescoes and stained-glass windows of churches, travelling, observing nature, etc.

What is new in the concept of lifelong education is the effort to systematize the various contributions of education, which are often confusing. This is particularly necessary at a time when the individual is overwhelmed with enormous floods of information and when there are more and more opportunities for education.

In the nineteenth century, the school, i.e. the formal and institutionalized instruction given to young people who were subject to discipline and rigid systems of selection, gained a monopoly of education. The school became compulsory and was considered the principal cause of the rapid progress of the industrialized societies. It was at school that young people were 'prepared for life'. Man's life was divided into three separate phases: school and learning—active life—old age. What was learned at school remained valid for a lifetime. Moreover, an individual's whole future life depended on his school record; it was at school that the game of individual destiny was played out, and almost always with marked cards. In the nineteenth century, the school—the promoter of progress and the place of social selection—managed to acquire incomparable prestige and became one of the most powerful of institutions, strictly administered and carefully protected against all outside interference. It is this prestige of the school, of public education, that in all countries of the world forms the greatest obstacle to any far-reaching reforms of education systems. As a consequence, it is in the sector of formal education that the realization of the concept of lifelong education finds the hardest problems to solve.

Historical background

The growth of the industrial society has created new educational needs, especially on the part of adults. In 1919, immediately after the First World War, the Adult Education Committee in the Ministry of Reconstruction of the United Kingdom described adult education, in a report which has since become famous, as being 'a permanent national necessity, an inseperable aspect of citizenship'. It concluded that opportunities for adult education should be 'both universal and life-long' [114, p. 14]. This report perhaps marks the date of birth of the term 'lifelong learning' [41, p. 19].

However, the conceptualization of the principle of lifelong education is more recent. It did not really begin until during the sixties.

The theoretical foundations were worked out during a period of barely ten years. The first publications of model systems of lifelong education appeared at the beginning of the seventies. Today, lifelong education is accepted everywhere as a basic principle which serves as a starting-point in all thinking about questions of general scope in the field of education and which is clearly behind all important educational reforms. At the present time, however, there is still not one country which has an over-all system of education planned entirely from the point of view of lifelong education.

Before trying to explain the meaning of lifelong education as clearly and simply as possible, we will have to go back to one special point in the history of its creation.

The concept of lifelong education is the result of international co-operation. It is the collective thinking and exchange of ideas and experiences between educators, research workers and administrators of various nationalities, conducted thanks to such organizations as Unesco and the Council for Cultural Co-operation (CCC) created by the Council of Europe, which have given birth to this revolutionary concept, and it is only thanks to this fact that it has conquered the whole world in just a few years, that is to say, almost instantaneously.

In December 1965, Unesco's International Committee for the Advancement of Adult Education considered a report by Paul Lengrand on the 'concept of continuing education, and recommended that Unesco should endorse the principle of lifelong education. This, it said, was the animating principle of the whole process of education, regarded as continuing throughout an individual's life from his earliest childhood to the end of his days, and therefore calling for integrated organization' [114, p. 7]. In the same year, 1965, one of the committees of the CCC discussed lifelong education and recommended that it be made the subject of a general debate. In 1967, the CCC decided to consider lifelong education as the principal guiding line in all its work in the field of education. It then began to prepare and publish an important series of studies on this subject. In 1968, Unesco's General Conference defined twelve objectives for International Education Year (1970): one of them was lifelong education. At that time, publications on the subject began to multiply. [1] An evaluation of the results of International Education Year showed that lifelong education had become one of the leading topics in the various projects carried out by

---

1. See bibliography contained in: R.H. Dave and N. Stiemerling, *Lifelong education and the school* [41, p. 127-54].

Unesco's Member States during the year [114, p. 7]. In 1971, the CCC noted that 'the conceptualization phase of lifelong education was closed', and in 1972, the principle of lifelong education was confirmed at the international level in the report of the International Commission on the Development of Education (presided over by Edgar Faure), entitled *Learning to be.* 'The Commission laid stress above all on two fundamental ideas: lifelong education and the learning society', as Edgar Faure says in the Preamble [54, p. xxxiii]. In 1975, however, the Rapporteur-General of the thirty-fifth session of the International Conference on Education had to state in his report: 'The concept of lifelong education has evolved during the last two decades. Although the concept has made some headway and many theoretical studies on the subject have been published, and although it is generally accepted and constantly referred to be everybody, the notion still remains somewhat vague, even for many specialists' [73, p. 13].

The meaning of the concept

To begin with, it is surprising that the concept of lifelong education should be considered obscure. After all, the basic idea is a simple one. What is complex about it is its application, the planning of the far-reaching educational reforms to which it points.

Starting from the observation that today the amount of knowledge acquired in school no longer stands up against the wear and tear of time and is therefore insufficient for a whole lifetime, it must be supplemented and brought up to date after reaching adulthood. Retraining and adult education in their various forms have become indispensable. School education must be supplemented by other possibilities and other forms of learning and training. But if all these different educational processes are to be as effective as possible, they must be co-ordinated and integrated in a single, comprehensive education system: lifelong education.

However, lifelong education must not be confused with adult education or with continuous education, as happens fairly frequently, and sometimes, incidentally, in order to monopolize the concept for special purposes. Adult education is only one aspect—although an important one—of a system of lifelong education. As for the idea of continuous training, it is also restrictive in that in relates exclusively to the vocational side of education, whereas in the concept of lifelong education, the term 'education' is understood in its broadest sense.

Lifelong education is also an answer to the criticisms directed at schools and institutionalized education in general. The traditional school systems find it difficult to adapt to the increasingly rapid changes characteristic of our time and respond poorly to the new educational needs which are arising. These changes, which are bringing about real mutations of societies in all parts of the world, have numerous causes. Presumably the most important of them is the explosive increase of scientific discoveries, technological progress and means of information, side by side in certain areas with the demographic explosion, as well as economic and political upheavals. The enormous increase of man's needs, the unbelievable diversity of occupations [1] and the rapid fluctuations of employment opportunities are consequences of this, and all of them affect problems of education.

It seems obvious that school instruction, which necessarily always remains limited in time to the phases of childhood and adolescence, will never be able to meet all the requirements of a changing world. Such a world calls imperiously for other possibilities and other forms of education, but it would be unjust to blame the schools for all the inadequacies of our education systems.

A world of constant change calls for flexible education systems. Education must remain constantly in movement and resort unceasingly to innovation. It is not so much the knowledge itself which counts, but rather the process of acquisition which becomes decisive. It is therefore neither 'having' nor 'being' which are the decisive factors but 'becoming'. In this context, it will be the responsibility of the schools to prepare young people not 'for life', taken as a specific whole, but for a continuous education. The primary role of the school will be to learn to learn, or, better still, to learn to become.

School systems, by their very nature, have a tendency to be rigid and resistant to change. Their traditionalism and their conservatism explain why voices from the educational world and society have been heard calling for the elimination of schools. To a certain extent, lifelong education echoes these arguments by challenging the educational monopoly which the schools are trying to preserve.[2] It also challenges the fact that, in many countries, practically all public funds

---

1. The *Canadian descriptive classification of occupations* gives information about 6,700 different careers [13, p. 46].
2. Incidentally, Ivan Illich was not the first to advance such arguments. Anatole France had already written: 'In my opinion, there is only one school which can form one's mind, and that is not to go to any school'.

spent for educational purposes—and these represent enormous sums—go to formal education, leaving practically nothing for non-formal education.

From the point of view of lifelong education, educational activity is conceived as a whole, and all sectors of education are integrated in a single, coherent system. But lifelong education is not a carefully detailed recipe which can be applied as it stands to all situations. It is a general directive, a guide and an outlook on which education systems should be built. This general concept must be adapted to the realities and needs of the societies concerned. An industrial nation has different needs than a developing nation. Wherever a large part of the population is illiterate, adult literacy constitutes an important side of any system of lifelong education. In a very advanced country, on the other hand, the problem of leisure may influence the establishment of such a system.

The concept of lifelong education offers a special opportunity to developing countries. Their school systems are not as deep-rooted, not as firmly established, not as rigid and petrified as those of the industrialized countries. It is easier for them to carry out a radical reform. Moreover, lifelong education will help them to rediscover their ancient educational methods based on observation and participation, which have been buried and forgotten because of the predominance of school systems which were often imported from abroad. In a certain sense, the idea of lifelong education may lead to a real educational renascence.

Lifelong education is also an ideology

It would be a mistake to think that the concept of lifelong education raises questions of an essentially administrative or structural order. The over-all integration of all educational sectors looking towards a coherent policy of educational action goes far beyond the problems of planning and organization.

Lifelong education is a genuine educational project. Like any project of this kind, it looks to the future: it envisages a new type of man; it is the carrier of a system of values; it involves a project of society. It constitutes a new philosophy of education. This project also contains political options. It is ideological. And it is a Utopia. However, as Bertrand Schwartz writes: 'This Utopia is, however, intended to be a practical proposition and we are not afraid to say that what we are offering is not speculation, but a plan of action, that it is a political tool which will allow us to choose today what we wish our future to be tomorrow' [131, p. 28].

From the point of view of its promoters, lifelong education is the only kind of education which could be suitable for modern man. For the man who is living in a world in transformation, in a society in mutation. Such a man must be able to adapt himself continuously to new situations. For this, he must be dynamic, possess imagination and be creative. In addition, he must be able to work in groups and tackle problems from an interdisciplinary point of view.

Lifelong education should guarantee every individual the full flowering of his personality. It would then be a powerful factor for democratization. Since it would be an over-all and homogeneous system, it would make it possible for an individual to resume his studies at any time or to enter into a sector of the system adapted to his abilities.

For some authors, education is no longer the characteristic of one phase of its existence, but 'a standard dimension of life' which effects a 'profound change in the individual's outlook and style of life' [56, p. 55]. It should not only lead to far-reachnig changes in society, but should also bring about a kind of continuous cultural revolution.

The concept of lifelong education also gives rise to certain fears, criticisms and opposition. Hermann H. Frese has entitled an article 'Permanent education—Dream or nightmare?' [57]. And at the thirty-fifth session of the International Conference on Education, the delegate from Brazil drew the assembly's attention to the fact that lifelong education might make the adult into an eternal minor. To those who fear that through lifelong education the existence of the individual human being would be invaded and encumbered by endless teaching, that it would herald the domination of school-teachers and that instead of living, acting and creating, man would be condemned to undergo the calvary of an unremitting apprenticeship; the defenders of this system reply that education must not be confused with school instruction and that as a part of lifelong education the teacher would change his attitude completely and become animateur or guide who would help to awaken unknown or sleeping abilities so that everyone could share in the happiness of all human beings who fulfil themselves completely.

Educational consequences

The concept of lifelong education presupposes a new pedagogy, adapted to the needs of our time. In a period characterized by transformations which are so rapid and far-reaching and in which science and technology are progressing at a constantly faster rate, encyclopaedic knowledge is obsolete; encyclopaedias are aging much faster than men. Education can no longer be restricted to a mere transmission of knowledge; pedogogy is once more finding its true dimensions.

To learn to learn, to learn to become—this calls for educational measures which will be more flexible, more dynamic, more open to the world and the surrounding environment, more individualized than mere learning. What is needed is to awaken motivation, curiosity and individual enthusiasm in the pupil. He must be induced to take his destiny as an educated person into his own hands. He must learn to work, to study, to invent, to create and no longer to memorize theories and facts. He should no longer undergo education but should participate fully in the educational process. He should be prepared for self-training and self-education. 'The individual not only learns passively what is presented to him by a teacher, he also assumes responsibility for the specific orientation and organization of his own education' [56, p. 66].

Self-management in education is only possible when there is also self-evaluation. The pupil must be prepared to act as the judge of his own abilities, progress and defects. Only in this way will he be able, once he is an adult, to make a rational choice, among the various possibilities of education and training open to him, of those which are suited to his needs and abilities. Obviously, he will have to be helped, guided and directed in this process.

The theory of lifelong education starts from a vision of the oneness of educational problems. This systematic approach is also reflected in the new pedagogy. Since the phenomena and problems of the world are also of a global nature, they call for a multidisciplinary approach if they are to be understood. Education will have to be conceived from this point of view if it is to meet real needs and situations.

From what has been said above, it is clearly evident that lectures seem to be a thing of the past. The educator's role is changing: instead of a teacher, he is becoming an animateur, often working together with his colleagues in other disciplines (team-teaching). Traditional classes are beginning to break up and are being replaced by study groups in which the pupils work together on selected problems in common agreement with the teachers. They no longer learn things by heart, but learn to use all means of information, from libraries, radio and television to computers. They learn by working, with their teachers and among themselves, in school and out of school.

This renovated pedagogy, which is in keeping with the concept of lifelong education, is an active and liberating pedagogy which encourages personal initiative and creativity and is aimed at the complete fulfilment of each individual. At the same time, it is a collective enterprise in which the entire community takes part.

Models

Several models of a system of lifelong education have recently been worked out. They all resemble each other. We shall try to give as brief a summary of them as possible.

What is proposed by the concept of lifelong education is an over-all system of education which is coherent and continuous but none the less structured. In it, we can distinguish various sectors which correspond to the different stages of life and, to a large extend, to the traditional educational structures. What are changing are their contents and their articulation.

At the threshold of the system, we find the education provided by the parents and the nursery schools. *Pre-school education* occupies an especially important place in a system of lifelong education. It is the most decisive period for shaping the personality. As we shall see further on (p. 85-7), it is also a privileged place for effective democratization, for it is probably there that the encouragement of equality of opportunity in education runs the greatest risks.

What are developed during the phase of pre-school education are, first, pyschological independence and, secondly, the socialization of the child, who becomes accustomed, while playing, to entering into relations with others and to group activities. The basic language mechanisms are developed and the child can become familiar with written language. He elaborates on his elementary perceptions of the outside world. In addition, pre-school education can encourage the development of creativity. While being neither too rigid nor pushing learning too far, pre-school education prepares the child for school. From the point of view of lifelong education, it is necessary to establish close links between pre-school and primary education. The two types of school ought not to be separated from the architectural point of view. The transition from one sector to the other should be as smooth as possible. In Sweden, for example, in the Malmö area, where primary school starts at the age of 7, '6 year old children spend

half-days in primary schools, while some primary school children
return for re-education activities to the nursery schools. In the Grenoble experiment in France... the teacher of the last year of nursery
school (5 years old in France) accompanies the group into the primary
school for the first two years, thus ensuring the maximum possible
continuity' [32, p. 10].

The pre-school phase is followed by a *basic school* or a *basic course
of studies*.

In a system of lifelong education in an industrialized country,
where the entire school sector is fully developed and where school
attendance is normally compulsory for children from 6 to 16 years, this
phase, according to Bertrand Schwartz, may be called 'basic school'.
It consists of two levels corresponding to the traditional primary
school and the first stage of the secondary school.

In the developing countries, where universal school attendance
exists only in exceptional cases, the practice for some time has been
to provide 'basic education', which is also understood to be the first
phase of a lifelong education. However, this basic education does not
necessarily have to be given in schools. It can be provided in the course
of non-formal educational activities, or as a result of a combination
of the two types. Since we are taking up the topic of basic education
in one of the following chapters (see p. 138-40), we shall concentrate
here on the 'developed' model, while emphasizing that this does not
involve any difference of principle but only a difference with respect
to the relative weight of school education as opposed to other forms
of education.

The basic school gives all pupils a common fund of essential
knowledge. This includes, first of all, the mastery of certain languages:
the mother tongue, one foreign language, mathematics; then the
foundations of scientific methodology and technique, civic and social
education, artistic education.

Besides this common fund, the pupil has the choice of a considerable number of options. The selection of these options, or rather
these educational objectives, is arranged between pupils and teachers.
In this way, education takes account of individual educational needs.
The interim or final examinations are replaced by a system of credits,
in accordance with which the pupil receives a certain number of units
for each educational objective achieved until he has a sufficient
number to obtain the diploma he wants. Units can also be acquired in
out-of-school activities. Systems of this kind are already in use in the
United States, Canada (see p. 108-9) and Sweden. In this way,

education can be individualized to such a point that not only are there no more traditional classes and 'levels' but even the schedules and curricula are no longer fixed. They are adjusted to the rate of progress of the pupils, who are free to organize their studies as they see fit. The work is done mainly in groups of various sizes, where pupils of different ages also mingle together. It is obvious that an organization of such flexibility calls for considerable and continuous efforts of guidance and evaluation on the part of those in charge. And the pupils must be genuinely motivated if they are to derive the maximum amount of benefit.

The choice between courses which lead either to higher studies or to vocational training is made at the end of the basic school.

In *vocational education*, detailed specialization is avoided, as it is impossible to make any long-term prediction of one's needs with respect to employment. It imparts a certain practical intelligence and develops aptitudes, especially those which will help one to be successful in refresher courses.

The keystone of the system is *adult education*. It occupies such an important place in a system of lifelong education that the two notions are often confused, which goes to show a total misunderstanding of the meaning of the concept of lifelong education. It is true that this concept was first conceived, worked out and disseminated in groups concerned with adult education. It is equally true that the sector of adult education, which, insofar as it relates to lifelong education, also comprises the entire tertiary and university sector, ought to be developed to the maximum extent, that it should offer adults a broad range of educational possibilities and multiple choices of continuous, refresher and remedial training courses, so as to help them to adjust to new job situations or to resume neglected studies, to participate in cultural activities or to make an intelligent use of their leisure. Lastly, it is also true that this sector, once it has been properly developed, takes on much more important dimensions than the others (after all, it concerns a stage of life that is normally four or five times longer than that spent in school). However, if lifelong education is limited to the post-school sector, its real meaning is completely lost. For the essential characteristic of a system of lifelong education is that there is no break anywhere, but rather continuity and integration everywhere, especially between the school and the post-school phase, between school and adult education. The important thing is that the school should open the way to the adult world and prepare young people for adult life, of which education is an intrinsic part.

From this point of view, the school is transformed into an educational and cultural centre, which serves the community as a whole. It is no longer an enclosed area, cut off from reality and reserved for only a fraction of the population. It is genuinely integrated into its community. Everybody meets there freely for various activities, everybody makes use of its installations.

In a system of lifelong education, the proper place for education is in the system as a whole. This means, among other things, that it should receive an adequate proportion of the public funds invested in education.

Towards realization of the goal

Nowhere in the world, except perhaps in China—and our information is too fragmentary to confirm this—has any system of lifelong education been completely realized. The achievement of this goal is extremely complex. The difficulty is due in part to the fact that non-institutionalized education is an important aspect of the system. Its integration in an institutionalized system is a contradiction in terms. For this reason, it will never be entirely possible to plan lifelong education, at least as long as there are non-governmental and spontaneous educational activities. In the majority of countries practically the whole out-of-school sector, and adult education in particular, is based on private or semi-governmental initiative.

However, a very large number of innovations and reforms are now being conceived from the point of view of lifelong education. Practically all the examples mentioned in this book are of this character and might be quoted in this chapter just as well as in others.

In Thailand, we have one very modest but significant example of a project carried out in the spirit of lifelong education [7]. Following a functional literacy campaign, it was found necessary to obtain reading material. First of all, it was decided to establish small reading centres or village libraries and to supply them with miscellaneous books, novels, etc. However, the peasants seldom visited them and showed little interest. The authorities then decided to change their tactics. From then on, reading material was only furnished to villages which had shown a real interest and built a small centre themselves. And it was no longer books that were provided but daily newspapers, so that the villagers would be induced to go to the centre every day. At the present time, these centres, which are visited regularly by an average of thirty adults and a large number of schoolchildren, have the following material: one national and one local newspaper; one rural newspaper on adult education (a bimonthly publication of the Adult Education Division); one newspaper published by a private foundation for persons who have just learned to read; five or six books for the same class of persons; bulletins of various associations, as well as a small library—provided that the centre's committee has expressly asked for it. These centres are so successful that they are becoming real lifelong education centres where young people and adults meet to attend courses, exchange experiences with each other and with the teachers, organize radio listener's clubs, seminars, experimental classes, etc.

The *ujamaa* villages in the United Republic of Tanzania [1] are centres which offer both adults and young people an opportunity for self-education, either with official facilities or by a number of non-institutionalized, semi-official or unofficial means. The primary school has been transformed into a community education centre and is the principal instrument of the adult education system. Its teachers act as instructors, animateurs and co-ordinators for the educational activities of young people and adults. In this way, the school is becoming a meeting-point which provides a solution for all the educational and training needs of the community, and does not limit itself to teaching children only.

In Latin America, countries like Costa Rica, Panama and Peru have greatly reformed their education systems as a whole, with a view to adult education.

Peru believes, like the United Republic of Tanzania, that the school system constitutes the best institutional base for co-ordinating out-of-school educational activities. The Peruvian system is based on the *nucleos educativos comunales* (NEC), the organization of which is described in greater detail in another chapter (see p. 160):

All the educative resources of a locality are co-ordinated and used in the manner most suited to its needs. The NEC is to provide for adults and children alike. It is to integrate formal schooling and out-of-school activities into a comprehensive educational process, using both the regular school facilities and teaching personnel and the out-of-school community facilities

---

1. The United Republic of Tanzania considers that development in rural areas can take place faster and more efficiently if the families, which are ordinarily settled in small scattered villages, get together to establish or organize larger villages which will constitute economic, social and political units: the *ujamaa* villages [78].

and people with knowledge and skill that they can place at the service of their fellows. The traditional school will play a key role in the activities of the NEC, but it will no longer retain its former isolation from the community. ... The NEC has indeed the potentiality of becoming the kind of basic centre of education outlined in the present model [114, p. 47-8].

Partial reforms along similar lines are to be found in Brazil, for example, where the procedure for transferring from non-formal to formal education, as well as the age limits for the different levels, have been made more flexible, and in Mexico, where the formalities for obtaining access to education have been liberalized. Systems of education loans have been introduced in Bolivia, Ecuador, Honduras and Mexico [87, p. 32-3].

In the Arab countries, some States have adopted an integrated planning of education which goes beyond the limits of school education and covers other forms of non-formal and out-of-school instruction. In several of them, there has been an expansion of the one-class school. These States believe that if this type of school succeeds in modernizing its programmes and methods, it can constitute one of the new formulas of primary education.

Another formula is that of the basic polytechnic school, which has been adopted by Algeria as the basis for a reorganization of its primary and intermediate education. As its name implies, this school associates studies with real life and with society. A similar formula has just been introduced by Democratic Yemen.

In these countries, one can see a clear tendency towards integrating the primary grades and the first stage of the secondary school, thus corresponding to the 'basic school' of the model. There, too, one can see a distinct trend in favour of the polytechnic school. During the seventies, several Arab countries have carried out experiments with over-all or integrated secondary schools ('comprehensive schools'). Iraq has decided to establish four schools of this type. Jordan already has two of them and intends to establish three more. Saudi Arabia established its first school of this kind in 1975, and studies along these lines are under way in Egypt. In Kuwait, a project for educational reform, dating from 1974, recommends the organization of secondary education in one unified, comprehensive school.

In the United Kingdom and in France (at Grenoble), a new type of primary school has been developed: the *école ouverte* (open school), which meets the criteria of a model of lifelong education in the form in which it has been presented. Examples of this kind of school were the subject of detailed studies in the 'Lifelong education' project of the Council for Cultural Co-operation attached to the Council of Europe, the purpose of which was to evaluate pilot experiments in the European countries. We are basing our description of these open schools on the reports of the executive group of the CCC project.[1]

When you enter an 'open school', you find the children, either in groups or alone, engaged in many different activities. They are reading, writing, drawing, playing music, looking after their animals or acting out plays. The whole school is at the pupil's disposal. He goes from the documentation centre to an office in a quieter place where he can work alone, to a room where the teacher will supervise a small group which is in need of help, to the big assembly hall where he will find all his friends to watch a film or discuss a problem of community life, to a carpentry shop which is open to adults and to which he can return after class hours. School is no longer exclusively in the school. The pupils leave it to study the surroundings, to carry out observations and experiments outdoors and to visit other institutions. In some schools, 'vertical' groups are established where pupils of different ages meet together. There, the most advanced or the most talented help the others. The advantage of these groups is that the youngest feel themselves pulled along and the oldest pushed along.

In these establishments, there are no individual desks or reserved places. Various tables are arranged all around the room for different activities. And there are many unusual objects and equipment to help them to learn to count, measure, paint, etc. There are reading corners with a lot of books, but practically no textbooks. The children handle these books even before they know how to read, look at the pictures, try to find words which they know and in this way finally learn to read, with the help of the oldest.

Sometimes the teacher sits at his desk and the children come up to consult him. But most of the time he moves around among the children, advising one about how to conduct his project, listening to another read a text out loud, talking to a third about one thing and another. The teachers collaborate in a group and every child will find at least one with whom he feels more in sympathy, so that tragedies of mutual misunderstanding will be avoided.

1. Besides these reports [31 and 36], see in particular Bertrand SCHWARTZ, *Permanent education*, an annex of which contains a description of a school of this kind [131, p. 225-9]. Some parts of our text are taken verbatim from these sources.

The school is open to the parents, who contribute their experience from practical life and bring with them something of the outside world, or who come there simply to use the school equipment.

The challenge of the 'open schools' and the self-education, assisted by the teachers, which is practised there may be summed up as follows: if a child is left to himself, he will *in fine*, acquire at least as much knowledge as in a school where he is forced to do everything; moreover, he will be fulfilled, he will develop his independence and creativity.

In a system of lifelong education, the problem of transitions from one level to another or from one sector to another calls for special attention. The authorities in the Federal Republic of Germany are particularly aware of this. This appears from the '75 report' of the federal Education Council [42]. The problem is particularly acute—but often not recognized—at the time when the child enters school [130]. The establishment of a separate grade between nursery school and primary school is under study in various European countries, and especially in the Federal Republic of Germany. This country is now carrying out, on a fairly wide scale, an important experiment concerning lifelong education in its *Gesamtschulen*, which correspond to the comprehensive schools in the United Kingdom. The results of this experiment are not yet known.

One example which is just as famous as the comprehensive school and which has also been imitated in many other countries is the 'Open University' in the United Kingdom, which will be discussed in a later section (see p. 61-3]. This is one of the numerous adult education projects which would fit in with an over-all system of lifelong education. In some cases, as, for example, in the USSR, adult education is strongly institutionalized and closely linked to the school system, and especially to vocational and technical education. In other cases, it is in the van of the search for new educational formulas. Among the especially remarkable achievements in this field, similar examples of which can be found in various parts of the world, mention should be made of the 'community schools' and 'community colleges', the latter of which, as opposed to the former, are exclusively reserved for adults.[1] (We shall find more special examples of establishments of this kind in other chapters: see p. 150-1).

---

1. A more detailed description will be found in John Lowe [81, p. 80-5], on whose work we have based the following passage.

The community schools are based on the following principles: the school should belong to the community and interact with it; it must be the focal centre of community affairs; it must remain open in the evenings, at weekends and during vacations, and adults should consider it natural to make use of the school's facilities throughout their lives. These schools are, depending on each case, provided with miscellaneous installations: libraries, workshops, an auditorium for plays and films, swimming pools, nurseries, dispensaries, etc. Besides its service to the ideal of lifelong education, the community school can be considered as the most satisfactory type of adult education institution for the following reasons: (*a*) it is economical, as it ensures the maximum utilization of exisiting resources; (*b*) it destroys the feeling of alienation from the school; (*c*) it facilitates the transition from school activities to young people's activities, as well as the transition from the latter to adult activities; (*d*) it encourages encounters between all age groups; (*e*) it can be administered autonomously by the local community.

The principal purpose of centres of popular education, which are reserved for adults, is to provide vocational and technical training and, in many cases, pre-university education. In the United States, in particular, they also give courses in general culture. Their success depends on how closely they are linked to the local community and on their ability to meet the needs felt by the population. One particular form taken by these centres can be found in the people's universities and workers' universities of the USSR, Yugoslavia and other European countries.

THE RENOVATION OF THE SCHOOL SYSTEM FROM THE POINT OF VIEW OF LIFELONG EDUCATION

The school, especially the primary school, will continue to be the basic element in the education system, at any rate in countries with a high level of school attendance. Where this system is seriously under developed, it is not impossible that other less institutionalized and more flexible forms than the school may become preponderant [28]. Even in this case, however, the school will continue to be an important element in the system. For this reason we shall revert in somewhat greater detail to the transformations which will be needed before it can really fit into a system of lifelong education.

One preliminary observation to bear in mind is that, in a system of lifelong education, the school does not hold a monopoly of education. It constitutes one stage in a process which begins before school age and continues much beyond it. As a result, there are educational activities which take place before, together with and after the school stage. The school must take this fact into consideration so that it can become an integral part of the whole. In other words, pre-school, out-of-school and post-school education, as well as everything which is non-formal education, should serve to influence the objectives, contents, methods, means and structures of school education.

Up to now, few systematic studies and little detailed research have been carried out on this subject, although interesting experiments are in progress in this field, as we have already noted. Basically, however, these examples are more in the nature of pragmatic measures, and sometimes almost even improvisations or tentative approaches— which by no means deprives them of their value and their extremely important character as pilot projects—or, in other words, they are actions which are the result of essentially pedagogic research and not of any systematic thinking about the broader field of lifelong education. Those responsible for these experiments are seeking primarily to improve the realities of school education as such rather than as an element in a broader system.

However, important projects are under way in an attempt to explain how to renovate the school in a system of lifelong education. Two of them seem to us particularly worthy of interest. First, there is the programme of the Unesco Institute for Education in Hamburg, which since 1972 has concentrated its long-term activities on, *inter alia*, an exploratory study on the concept of lifelong education and its implications for educational programmes, as well as for research. Secondly, the Council for Cultural Co-operation in Strasbourg is carrying on a vast project on lifelong education; the particular stage which is of interest to us here also began in 1972. They are evaluating a certain number of pilot experiments on the basis of an analytical grid which takes the form of a list of principles to be observed in a system of lifelong education. This grid, by the way, is not the result of a purely theoretical exercise; it has been revised several times in the light of the results of an analysis of the projects considered.

Neither one of these two projects has been completed at the present time. However, preliminary results which have already been published give some precise, although provisional, clues to the question

we are considering. Let us try, therefore, to point out a few of the
main trends in them.[1]

The two approaches taken by R.H. Dave of the Institute for Education and the executive group of the CCC (headed by Bertrand
Schwartz) are very different. The second is much more pragmatic and
analytical than the first. On the other hand, the first is more complete.
It includes almost all the aspects of educational planning. The grid
used by the Bertrand Schwartz group consists entirely of objectives.
Questions of methods, means, etc., are not dealt with in the explana-
tions except by implication. R.H. Dave's ideas are primarily centred
on how to initiate the process of lifelong education in the individual,
on what he calls the 'enhancement of educability', in other words,
on how to enable the individual to become an educated person
throughout his life and to accept education as an essential dimension
of his existence, while B. Schwartz and his group are also concerned
about the dimension 'democratization of education', which according
to them should be achieved through lifelong education.[2] They are
also aware of the fact that some of these principles might conflict
with each other. For example, total individualization would be incon-
sistent with the objective of 'equality of opportunity', which implies
a single, identical school for everybody, in which account would be
taken of differences which are to be reduced rather than emphasized.
It will be necessary, therefore, to give serious consideration to the
implementation of the various objectives.

The results of these two approaches are to a large extent similar,
sometimes complementary but not contradictory, the difference consisting primarily of where the emphasis is placed. A combination of
them would give approximately the following results:

1. Up to now, the Unesco Institute for Education has published four monographs
   under this programme. The first, written by R.H. DAVE, *Lifelong education
   and school curriculum* [39], contains one part entitled 'Some implications for
   school programmes', which is also included in the third monograph. We are
   basing our attempted summary on that part. Likewise, there is a whole series
   of documents describing the progress of the 'lifelong education' project of the
   CCC. Here, we are referring primarily to a text prepared by the director of
   the project (Bertrand SCHWARTZ), entitled: *Grille d'analyse révisée: explication
   des hypothèses* [132].

2. In our opinion, it is quite possible to imagine a system of anti-democratic
   lifelong education, but not perhaps any real democratization without lifelong
   education.

School model in a system of lifelong education: objectives

The first objective mentioned by R.H. Dave concerns the awareness of the need for lifelong education. The learner has to realize that the world in which he lives is one characterized by rapid change; he has to realize that school education cannot mean the completion of education, that it is his responsibility to participate in progress, in his own interest and that of society. For the B. Schwartz group, the touchstone of lifelong education is the development of active attitudes towards education and, through this, towards activity in daily life. For that purpose, it is necessary to encourage the self-fulfilment of the learner and eliminate boredom in the school; it is also necessary to develop his sense of independence, to instil in him the feeling that he is responsible for his own education, and to link the subjects of learning as closely as possible to real life.

R.H. Dave's second objective consists of increasing 'educability'. Instead of stressing the teaching of specific knowledge in various fields, it is more important to develop learning mechanisms. The learner must acquire the habit of using different learning strategies: learning under the guidance of a teacher, without a teacher and in small groups where the roles of learner and teacher are reversed. He must learn to observe, to listen, to express himself, to ask questions and to reason. He must become capable of identifying himself with his educational needs and to plan, conduct and evaluate his own studies.

In addition, the Schwartz group emphasizes the importance of individualizing the rate at which knowledge and know-how are acquired. It stresses the relativity of the independence of the pupil, who, while left free to find his own means and resources by himself, should always be helped and guided by the teacher. It also stresses the importance of 'action', which should replace learning based solely on knowledge by tasks which have to be carried out ('knowledge is not really acquired until one is capable of making real use of it'). It is also such 'action' that will provide a real motivation for education.

R.H. Dave describes the third objective as 'exposure to broad areas of learning'. The pupil should acquire as broad a base as possible and have a wide range of choices in pursuing his studies. He should become familiar with nature and with the structure of the different disciplines rather than with their contents, and with their essential elements, especially their language and concepts. In this way he acquires the tools of learning which he needs in order to advance in different fields, identifies his own interests and enters on the path towards his own creative self-fulfilment.

The Schwartz group is working against the encyclopaedism of the traditional school and seeks to replace it by a more detailed study of certain limited but multidisciplinary fields. The so-called pedagogy of content is to be replaced by the so-called pedagogy of 'objectives'. What is necessary is to bring different fields of knowledge together and compare them with each other, so as to derive from them common methods and principles and give them new dimensions.

A fourth objective which is found in both approaches is to link up school and out-of-school experiences, or to integrate different educational situations. The experiences in both sectors have a tendency to reinforce each other. Accordingly, it is important that young people should not only profit by the different opportunities offered to them but should also learn to take an active part in them. In this way, they will come to know themselves better and understand the kind of part they can play in private life as well as in society.

The development of equality of opportunity is a central objective for the Schwartz group. This objective may be subdivided as follows: to develop pre-school education and early childhood centres; to permit everyone to progress at his own rate ('don't hold back the most brilliant/help the weakest'); to help those who have some difficulties and not to drop them; to delay definitive choices; to permit and facilitate second choices. We shall revert to this problem at some length in a later chapter.

Contents of the programme

Syllabuses should be flexible and constitute a broad base for subsequent studies. With regard to the elementary school, young children should be able to acquire a common fund of knowlegde, so that they will not find their progress blocked in the course of their education. What should be cultivated above all are the instrumental subjects and languages. The centre of interest should shift from subjects of specific knowledge, which may quickly become obsolete, to the structural aspects of disciplines; in other words, the pupil should be given solid points of departure and the necessary tools for future studies. It is essential to link educational experiences to real life and to the exploration of the environment and milieu to which the pupils belong. 'The more a pupil can be motivated to acquire knowledge which will enable him to decipher the world, the more be will be bored by learning things for which he sees no purpose', says B. Schwartz.

Another essential point is to link up and combine studies with practical work. The pupil should get into the habit of making work his principal tool for enriching his learning and widening his horizon. The development of creativity is also important.

The pupil should learn to work by himself and, at a more advanced stage, he should be able to make a free choice among his centres of interest and to plan and carry out his studies himself.

Methods and means

In the first place, it is necessary to develop independent work. The learner must become autonomous and confident in his ability to learn by himself. As Dave says, 'Every learner [should become] his own teacher'.

The techniques of reciprocal learning should be used to a large extent, so that young people will stimulate and help each other as much as possible. In order to be able to work in groups, the pupil must be trained to express himself, to listen to others and to be considerate of others. If there is undoubtedly one requirement for instruction in guided groups, it is that the assistance and support of the teachers should be gradually reduced as the pupils make progress and become more mature. To an increasing extent, they must be trusted with responsibility and initiative for planning and organizing their own studies.

It is necessary to make maximum use of all the facilities provided by modern educational technology. In this context, we must emphasize the importance of knowing how to handle and master the mass media.

Evaluation procedures

At the learner's level, a radical renovation of evaluation procedures is absolutely necessary. The primary purpose of evaluation should no longer be to establish a process of selection, of bringing about repetitions and failures—which are extremely expensive for the community and frustrating for the individuals concerned—but should be to guide and help them to make progress. Evaluation must become a formative function. For this, it will have to become more flexible and, above all, it will have to be combined with self-evaluation. The pupil, therefore, will have to be able to participate in guiding and directing himself. Evaluation will have to be linked to a system of credits.

However, continuous evaluation is also necessary at the level of the system itself, which will have to be periodically challenged, with the participation of all concerned, and evaluated with respect to the precise objectives which have been assigned to it. Lifelong education calls for a lifelong critical evaluation of education and its systems.

Structures

From our account of a school model which is an integral part of the broader framework of lifelong education, it naturally follows that this school will not be an isolated institution, separated from its environment and from the community. It will integrate itself vertically with all the other stages of education; it will provide a basic education, especially at the primary level, which will subsequently be diversified and enriched, either at the higher levels of institutionalized education or in the various forms of post-school education. In any case, school will no longer be considered as leading to a definitive end. Consequently, we must not try to meet the increased needs of education and training by prolonging compulsory schooling, but rather by strengthening and broadening the possibilities of informal education.

The horizontal integration of this system is achieved by ensuring mobility between levels of education, between situations in education, work and leisure, and by integrating education into working life.

It is obvious that the realization of such a model would have important repercussions on the role and training of teachers.

RECURRENT EDUCATION

'Education is a subject much given to vogues, and in vogue at the moment is "recurrent education"', writes Mark Blaug in one of his recent books [10, p. 72]. After all, we are now experiencing a proliferation of models in the field of education, a symptom that the crisis of the system has not yet been overcome.

The concept of recurrent education, which was introduced at the end of the sixties, and preached in particular by the OECD, has quickly found a wide and continuous response and aroused much interest in both the industrialized and the developing countries. In

1975, it was the topic of a Conference of European Ministers of Education [135].

Recurrent education is a system which essentially concerns adults and which can find its proper place in the more general framework of lifelong education. The Conference of European Ministers of Education even went so far as to formulate the following statement: '[Recurrent education] forms an indispensable part of the broader socio-economic and cultural policies for translating the concept of permanent education into practice' [CME/HF(75)12, Resolution 1].

Various authors have given slightly different definitions of recurrent education, but its basic principle is simple: it amounts to introducing a 'sandwich' system in which every individual would have an opportunity to resume his studies or training after they had been interrupted, and in this way to alternate periods of work (or leisure) with periods of education throughout his life [109, p. 7; 136, p. 5].

This principle can be interpreted in a flexible way, as shown by Diagram 1, which represents five variants of its application now under study in Sweden. It is easy to imagine others, in which an initial period of work would begin, for example, just after compulsory schooling or after the acquisition of a 'basic education'.

Recurrent education is a concrete articulation of the concept of lifelong education. For this reason, all considerations of a general nature concerning lifelong education, and especially those relating to the necessary renovation of school systems and pedagogy, remain relevant from the point of view of recurrent education. However, the latter concept is more explicit in the post-school field, which is its real field of application. The idea of alternation is a practical scheme which does not follow automatically from the theory of lifelong education.

Like lifelong education, recurrent education has actually existed for a very long time. However, a student who had interrupted his studies for one reason or another would find many difficulties if he wanted to resume them. It is very difficult to jump onto a moving train once one has left it. With recurrent education, this would become common practice.

There are many reasons which militate in favour of introducing a system of recurrent education. The first is one of equity. The European governments which are interested in this doctrine are animated chiefly by a sense of equity. By offering a second or third chance, recurrent education could undoubtedly make an effective contribution to equality in education. However, this system offers still other important advantages: it creates closer ties between education and the

DIAGRAM 1.   Some possible models of recurrent education studied in Sweden.

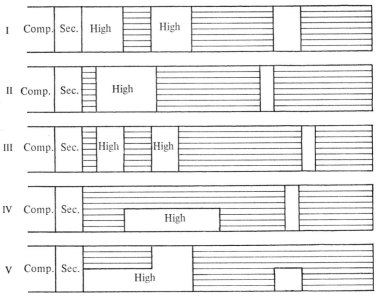

Comp. = Compulsory schooling   White spaces: studies

Sec.   = Secondary education,   Shaded spaces: work
           second cycle

High   = Higher education

Model I: Higher education directly follows the second stage of secondary
           education. It comprises two study periods separated by one period of
           vocational activity. After working for a few years in an occupation,
           this model provides for a brief study period, which may consist of a
           refresher or advanced course.

Model II: Direct transition from secondary education to professional activity,
           after which higher education is provided uninterruptedly. Refresher
           course later in life.

Model III: Periods of vocational activity both after secondary education and bet-
           ween periods of higher education. Refresher or advanced courses later.

Model IV: Part-time higher studies. These studies begin after an active period
           following secondary education.

Model V: Part-time higher studies beginning at the same time as professional life,
           immediately after secondary education. The last level of higher educa-
           tion is full time.

Source: Jarl BENGTSSON, *Recurrent education: the Swedish point of view* [135c,
p. 43]. See also: Mark BLAUG [10, p. 73] and Vladimir STOIKOV [129, p. 4].

working world; it enables young people to enter active life more quickly and, in general, to assume adult responsibilities; it permits education to be better adapted to the requirements of the labour market; it relieves the pressure on higher education caused by the broadening of the secondary system, a source of well-known difficulties (*numerus clausus*, etc.); it also helps somewhat to narrow the educational gap which is forming between generations (see Diagram 2).

DIAGRAM 2.   Forecasts of the composition of the Swedish population in 1980 with respect to education.

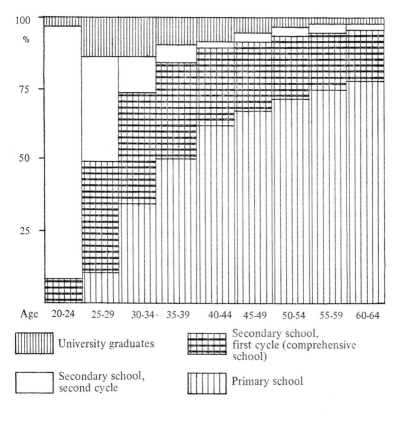

Source : Jarl BENGTSSON, *Recurrent education : the Swedish point of view* [135c, p. 48].

In addition, the effectiveness of higher education is likely to increase if it is imparted to really motivated adults who have acquired some degree of maturity rather than to young people who are taking courses either because they do not know what else to do or cannot find a job.

In addition to long-term planning, the establishment of a system of recurrent education calls for certain preliminary steps, such as the introduction of the right to leave for study and training, modular study programmes, evaluation and admission procedures for higher studies which have been renovated along the lines of a system of credits.

As in the case of lifelong education, there is no country in the world today which has set up a complete system of recurrent education. However, there are some countries which have enacted interesting legal provisions which constitute a partial realization of this system. However, it is almost always rather difficult to single them out among all those which relate to lifelong education.

In the Eastern European countries, part-time studies (see Model IV in Diagram 1) are very common and constitute an important and well-established part of the higher education systems in those countries. Different schemes exist side by side: night courses, correspondence courses, outside studies (where the student has no contact with the university except for selecting his courses of study and for taking his examinations).

In Poland, for example, during the academic year 1974/75, only 60 per cent of the students enrolled in higher education were attending full-time courses. In all those countries, students who combine their studies with work enjoy special advantages (paid leave, free transportation to their place of study, etc.).

In Yugoslavia, certain faculties have introduced modular programmes: the complete four-year programme is divided into four parts, each one of which leads to a special diploma. This country also offers the possibility of combining full-time studies with part-time studies.

The idea of recurrent education was probably born in Sweden (119o, p. 511-23]. The Swedish Commission of Education, founded in 1968, published its first analysis of these problems in 1969 under the title (in Swedish): *Higher education, its functions and structures,* and, likewise in 1969, Olof Palme, then Minister of Education, described the principles of recurrent education to his European colleagues at a conference held at Versailles. As a result, this country is making considerable efforts to make the concept of recurrent education a reality. It has consequently reformed its secondary sector, it has revised its university entrance requirements (see p. 114-16), it is conducting information campaigns aimed at encouraging workers to undertake new studies, it is developing adult education, and negotiations are under way concerning the question of study leave.

In France, the Act of 1971 on lifelong education has established recurrent education in that country. This Act contains provisions concerning paid leave for studies, State financial assistance for persons attending retraining courses, pre-vocational courses, courses for career advancement, etc.

In 1973, Belgium adopted similar legislation, the so-called Day Release Law. This gives worker/students an opportunity to be compensated from their working time for the hours passed in post-school education, without any loss of pay. This law applies to all workers of less than forty years of age—with the exception of teaching staff and workers employed in the public services—and who are attending courses organized or subsidized by the State. This law was given additional force in 1974: the benefit of day release was given to workers enrolled in the first year of teaching in social advancement (evening or week-end courses in technical and vocational training), in university level courses (long type) and general education courses 'with a view to encouraging the economic, social and cultural advancement' of the people concerned.[1]

The alternation of theoretical work with practical work is now a universal principle in the People's Republic of China. Young people who have finished their secondary studies are obliged to enter active life and have to put in at least two years of practical work before they can be appointed by the community where they work to continue higher studies.

In countries where education systems are still greatly underdeveloped, it is hard to conceive of a completely organized system of recurrent education. On the other hand, there are many compensatory systems in which educational and training situations, or parts of them, are 'postponed' and not provided until after periods of practical activity. The most important form of 'deferred' education is adult literacy.

---

1. See Belgium's report presented at the thirty-fifth session of the International Conference on Education, p. 80-1.

Critical evaluation

Such authors as Mark Blaug and Vladimir Stoikov [1] have attempted to evaluate the effectiveness, and particularly the economic effectiveness, of a system of recurrent education. Their conclusions tend to regard this system with some caution. From the economic point of view, the deferment or prolonged postponement (more than five years) of certain branches of education is not a sound procedure, for the simple reason that money invested in educating an older person will not yield a return for as long a time as an investment in a young person. If there is only a two or three years' interval between the completion of secondary education and the beginning of higher education, the gains in experience and maturity, and consequently the reduced risk of choosing the wrong courses, can largely offset the disadvantages of the delay. Brief periods of alternation between studies and practical work can also be considered advantageous.

Training given to adults of a certain age is not *a priori* an economic loss. Retraining is almost always profitable and, in particular, it can help to overcome problems of structural unemployment. In developing countries, where a large part of the adult population has not received any formal schooling, it may be particularly worthwhile to provide remedial education and training. Certain successful projects in functional literacy are a proof of this.

The same authors have also expressed doubts about the possibility of reducing inequalities by a system of recurrent education. Experience shows that it is mainly those who have already reached a high level who profit by it. In such a system, therefore, inequalities would tend rather to become more pronounced.

There is a danger that recurrent education—like any lifelong education—may degenerate into a continuous educational activity and into a constant, uninterrupted race to climb the steps of the long ladder which leads to the higher stages of the educational and social system.

Vladimir Stoikov concludes his critical study of recurrent education with the following sentence: 'If not introduced with considerable preparation and care, it may only make the whole educational system an even more unmanageable colossus than it already is' [136, p. 115].

---

1. Mark BLAUG, *Education and the employment problem in developing countries* [10, p. 72-6]; and Vladimir STOIKOV, *The economics of recurrent education and training* [136].

THE ROLE OF THE MASS COMMUNICATION MEDIA

Lifelong education, which breaks down the barriers between the different sectors of teaching and education and tries to individualize the different forms of learning, as well as to free the individual from the constraints of excessively rigid educational structures, is obviously looking for new means and technologies in keeping with its aspirations. The mass communication media very naturally provide an answer to this need. It is not surprising, therefore, that these media are very widely used in projects and activities aimed at establishing, at least partially, a system of lifelong education. There are many examples of experiments of this kind, only a few of which we can single out here.

At the beginning of 1970, the 'Open University' began to function in the United Kingdom. As its name indicates, this is a university which is open to all. The only admission requirement is a minimum age of 21. This university awards two different diplomas upon completion of the studies, the B.A. and the B.A. Honours degrees, which are equivalent to the similar certificates of other university institutions. Besides being open to all, what distinguishes it from other universities is the fact that the student is not obliged to attend lectures at certain fixed hours, to follow courses, listen to a teacher or participate in exercises. The courses are given at home, by mail, by radio and by television, and the student is free to arrange his own study schedule. In order to receive a diploma, he has to earn a certain number of credits. Each of these credits corresponds to a one-year course and requires thirty-two weeks of work, of ten to fourteen study hours each. There is a very wide range of choices: ninety. At the present time, the courses consist of weekly radio and television broadcasts, as well as work packages sent by mail containing texts, explanatory notes, comments on the respective radio or television broadcasts, and in some cases equipment for carrying out experiments, exercises for self-evaluation and lessons to send in. Every student is advised and supervised by a tutor, who is located in one of the 260 study centres distributed throughout the country. At these centres, the student meets his tutor and his colleagues to exchange experiences or to work in groups. The centres also contain different kinds of technical equipment with which, for example, they can listen to or watch earlier broadcasts or use a computer. Once a year, the students attend a course of one or two weeks as residents in a university centre. The constant evaluation of the student's work is supplemented by examinations.

The Open University, therefore, offers a combination of different methods of long-distance education, systematically integrated with each other and supplemented by a system of personal and continuous guidance and evaluation. This university is designed as a 'second chance' system. At the present time, it is not yet possible to determine whether it really achieves this purposes. By the beginning of 1976, 50,000 students were enrolled in these courses, but up to now the number of working-class students has been relatively low, thus confirming a familiar trend in adult education as a whole.

The example of the Open University has been followed in many industrialized and developing countries. In 1972, for example, a system of limited scope was established in Mauritius, called the 'College of the Air' and mainly connected, at first, with vocational training. Instruction is given in the form of correspondence courses, with accompanying printed and illustrated material, radio broadcasts and occasional meetings between teachers and students.

The Federal Republic of Germany has established the 'Diff', France the 'Ofrateme', the Netherlands 'Teleac', Sweden the 'Tru', Switzerland the 'Tele Kolleg', etc.

In 1972, Iran established an 'Open University' [3, p. 25] for students who were officially selected and enrolled throughout the year. Lessons are given by radio, television and correspondence, but the students can visit the university during the summer vacations or at any other time and receive practical training, work in laboratories, obtain advice and take examinations.

The 'People's Open University' was established in Pakistan in 1974. Its teaching methods are similar to those of the British Open University: a multimedia system consisting of programmed correspondence courses, combined with radio and television broadcasts, films, cassettes and tutorials in the study centres. This People's Open University gives two different kinds of course: a so-called 'functional education' programme and an advanced studies programme. The former is intended for children, young people and adults who have not gone to school. The programme of the second type is intended for college graduates, such as teachers or technicians living in rural areas and the educated unemployed, in order to prepare them to participate more fully in national development.

The functional education courses include the following: elementary literacy and learning practical know-how, vocational instruction in handicrafts, industry and trade, and rural education, concentrating primarily on the modernization of agriculture. The advanced studies programmes are devoted, among other things, to education, agriculture, technology, sciences and languages.

The system as a whole is consciously designed from the point of view of lifelong education and provides for close co-ordination with institutions of formal education.

In 1971-72, the University of Mindanao, in the Philippines, established a 'University of the Air'. This is not a multimedia system, for the courses are given solely by radio and the only printed aids are packages of reference books which are circulated among the students. This institution is intended especially for teachers and college graduates living in rural areas who wish to continue higher studies leading to an M.A. degree. Apart from their individual work, the participants in these courses meet regularly in schools located in different parts of the country, where they meet the teacher responsible for their particular course, discuss the broadcasts they have listened to and work in groups.

In Japan, preparations are under way to establish a 'university of the air' copied from the British Open University. A particularly new kind of experiment, however, is just being started in India. This is a programme intended for 96,000 primary school-teachers who teach science in rural areas. The programme is presented according to the usual multimedia scheme: radio, television, printed matter, personal guidance and direction. It is planned to use the telecommunication satellite to broadcast television programmes.

A slightly different system is being used in the Republic of Korea, where a programme of secondary education was launched in 1974 especially intended for young people who have left school prematurely, as well as for adults, particularly workers, who wish to add to their knowledge. This programme functions in the following way: the students are given semi-programmed manuals and listen to a one-hour broadcast every day of the week in both the morning and the afternoon. Every two weeks, they spend Sunday in school, where they are taught by secondary-level teachers. At present, there are 40 schools of this kind in operation, with an enrolment of 20,000 students.

Radio plays a paramount role in the education of adults living in rural areas. It is a powerful means of promoting rural development. At present, there are approximately 400 programmes all over the world aimed at farmers and other primary producers. There are many countries where 'listening groups' have been organized, composed of about thirty persons and guided by some responsible individual who has been appointed by his peers and is often trained for this task.

This system seems to be particularly well adapted to Africans: it can be found, in fact, in Burundi, the Central African Empire, Chad, Ethiopia, Ghana, Ivory Coast, Senegal, the United Republic of Cameroon, the United Republic of Tanzania, Zaire, etc.

An unusual form of this rural radio education is found in Senegal under the name of 'Disoo'. In this programme, which is broadcast entirely in Wolof, the language spoken by the majority of Senegalese and understood by almost all of them, the talking is done by the peasants themselves rather than by those in charge of the broadcasts. They ask questions, discuss their problems, talk about their experiences, criticize the broadcasts and especially measures taken by the authorities or the administration. 'Thus educational radio has become the instrument of a kind of direct democracy which no one, at least in Senegal, underestimates,' as Jean-Pierre Clerc says [119k, p. 574-8].

One multimedia programme which comes under the heading of adult education is the *Acción Cultural Popular* (ACPO) in Colombia [28, p. 52]. This is a combination of radio broadcasts, intended for poor *campesinos* of all ages, and cheap printed texts, aimed at encouraging literacy and providing a basic education. It appeals to a large number of volunteers, who look after those who follow this programme.

In recent times, television has often been used in schools, especially in connexion with the major programme in the Ivory Coast, where the entire education system is being transformed into a television system which will finally become a complete system of lifelong education. This ambitious project was designed to solve the urgent problem of universal school attendance. By 1980, there will be 20,000 television sets installed in all the schools, constituting a nation-wide network.

In those Ivory Coast schools which are already connected to the system, the whole basic material for class work is transmitted by television. The teacher becomes an animateur who uses this teaching material together with his class. The contents and quality of it depend entirely on the nerve centre of the system: the Bouaké television station.

An over-all five-year programme to evaluate this whole experiment has just been started. It is being carried out under the academic and scientific sponsorship of the Laboratory of Experimental Pedagogy of the University of Liège (Belgium). In view of the broad scope of the Ivory Coast experiment and the fact that several other countries are proceeding along similar lines, the results of this evaluation will be of the greatest interest, extending far beyond the borders of the country itself.

The Ivory Coast project began with the gradual introduction of television, commencing with the first grade of primary school. In 1968, another country, El Salvador, introduced teaching by television in secondary school, i.e. for classes 7 to 9. This experiment is significant because the introduction of instructional television (ITV) has been combined with a general reform of the school system. In this context, educational television has clearly acted as a catalyst in the reform. The operation seems to have been a success. 'Reform classrooms with ITV, retrained teachers, a revised curriculum, and new materials proved to be a better learning environment than either traditional classrooms or classrooms with all elements of the reform except for television' [119l, p. 123]. The introduction of ITV has made it possible to increase considerably the number of students in the secondary level without impairing the quality of the teaching, and at the same cost per student, or even less.

Recently, a report on higher education in the United States expressed the opinion that the development of the technology of communication constituted, in the field of education, 'the first great technological revolution in five centuries' [118].

The few examples taken from these countries show how the new mass communication media are slowly entering the field of education. It is to be expected that in the long run they will completely revolutionize the traditional education systems. Thanks to these media, education is freeing itself from the constraints of time and space. It is no longer confined to the school and taught at certain fixed times. A movement away from the school has begun.

Since these media are able to transmit knowledge and instruction to the farthest corners of the earth, is it perhaps possible that education will really become common property, available to all? Universal education seems to be within its grasp.

As the few examples already mentioned go to show, the education provided by multimedia systems makes it possible to individualize learning, gives individuals a free choice of the studies they wish to follow and a sense of responsibility for managing their own education throughout their lifetime. In other words, multimedia education meets the requirements of real lifelong education.

However, the mass communication media are not a 'neutral' tool—no educational tool is. As very clearly shown by the experiments in the Ivory Coast and El Salvador, the introduction of television in education is modifying the educational situation, the role of the teachers, etc. But what is particularly important, the existence of the mass media is also bringing about an integration of the different sectors of education and their methods. In other words, these media not only provide the technical means for achieving a system of lifelong education, but once they are started in such a process, they accelerate it.

Moreover, whether the official systems of education like it or not, radio, and especially television, are powers in education which are making themselves felt and changing educational assumptions. The great majority of children pass hours every day listening to their transistors or watching television. For this reason, these media have already created a parallel system of education. Obviously, this system is far from satisfactory. The exasperating mediocrity of it is often rightly criticized. It would seem urgently necessary to work out and implement policies aimed at integrating, or at least co-ordinating, our systems or information and education. The opportunities which such a step could offer are enormous. This being said, it is obvious that we cannot expect any miracles from mass communication media : they are only tools whose efficiency depends on the use which people make of them.

There is one last point which is deserving of mention. In recent years, several 'feasibility' studies have been made concerning the creation of regional systems of televised education [75; 149]. This opens up entirely new prospects: the internationalization of education —teaching which goes beyond ordinary borders.

THE CAMPAIGN AGAINST ILLITERACY

From Tehran to Persepolis

'All our ills come from illiteracy', as a distinguished participant [1] in the World Congress of Ministers of Education on the Eradication of Illiteracy exclaimed in 1965. The principal merit of that Tehran Conference was to draw the attention of world opinion to the scandal of illiteracy. In addition, it confirmed the concept of functional literacy,

---

1. Dr. Mohamed el Fasi, at that time Chairman of Unesco's Executive Board, in his closing speech.

...which implies more than the rudimentary knowledge of reading and writing that is often inadequate and sometimes chimerical. Literacy instruction must enable illiterates, left behind by the course of events and producing too little, to become socially and economically integrated in a new world where scientific and technical progress call for ever more knowledge and specialization. . . . Literacy work should not be regarded as an end in itself, but as an indispensable means of promoting the general, harmonious development of the illiterate masses.[1]

The Experimental World Literacy Programme (EWLP) was launched after the Tehran Conference. It involved a series of pilot projects carried out in eleven countries, mainly for the purpose of testing the concept of functional literacy. These projects were financed by the United Nations Development Programme (UNDP) and carried out under the auspices of Unesco. There were also a few additional projects, financed from other sources, but they were not included in the final evaluation.

An important chapter in the history of the campaign against illiteracy was closed with the publication of a critical evaluation of the results of EWLP [53], and with an International Symposium for Literacy held at Persepolis in September 1975. The *Declaration of Persepolis* is the reply given to the resolutions of the Tehran Conference after a decade of experimentation and efforts. It sums up the present phase of the problem of illiteracy.

Functional literacy in practice

The concept of functional adult literacy, combining a basic education (reading, writing, arithmetic—corresponding approximately to the fourth or fifth grade of school) with practical training, is generally known. However, in order to give a more exact idea of it, we shall briefly describe two of the EWLP projects: one was carried out in Algeria, the other in Iran.

In Algeria, the project was centred around civic education, in the broad sense of the term, and social development. What they had in mind, in particular, were attitudes towards society and motivations which would encourage increased production. The objectives, therefore, were primarily of a political nature and were aimed at integrating the efforts of the individual in the development plans of the nation.

1. World Congress of Ministers of Education on the Eradication of Illiteracy, Tehran, 8-19 September 1965, *Final report*, paras. 41, 42.

DECLARATION OF PERSEPOLIS

The number of illiterates is constantly growing.

This reflects the failure of development policies that are indifferent to man and to the satisfaction of his basic needs.

In spite of the progress made in some countries as a result of far-reaching social changes, there are close to one thousand million illiterates in the world, and many more under-nourished people.

In many cases, moreover, even people who have become literate have not yet acquired to a sufficient degree the means of becoming aware of the problems of the societies in which they live and of their own problems, nor the means of solving them or of playing a real part in their solution. . . .

Successes were achieved when literacy was linked to meeting man's fundamental requirements, ranging from his immediate vital needs to effective participation in social change. . . .

Tribute should be paid to those mass campaigns that have already brought about the complete or almost complete eradication of illiteracy in certain countries and to regional or more limited experiments, which have helped to prepare innovative methods with regard to the programming, means and organization of literacy activities linked to development aims. These experiments, and in particular functional literacy programmes and projects, have made a valuable contribution to the common stock of practical methods in the field of literacy and basic education. Greater use should be made of them in future efforts.

The International Symposium for Literacy, meeting in Persepolis from 3-8 September 1975, in unanimously adopting this Declaration, considered literacy to be not just the process of learning the skills of reading, writing and arithmetic, but a contribution to the liberation of man and to his full development. Thus conceived, literacy creates the conditions for the acquisition of a critical consciousness of the contradictions of society in which man lives and of its aims; it also stimulates initiative and his participation in the creation of projects

Continued on page 70

Special emphasis was placed on community life, co-operatives and State enterprises.

Literacy groups were formed in both the agricultural and the industrial sectors. Approximately 54,000 illiterate persons participated in the project, nearly half of whom successfully completed the two course cycles of twenty to twenty-two months, with four sessions of one-and-a-half hours weekly. The learning of reading, writing and arithmetic was completely integrated in the presentation and discussions of the study topics. The subjects dealt with were presented on posters or in films and discussed later in groups.

Among the questions dealt with, we might mention the following by way of example: Why learn to read?—The worker should train himself for promotion—Our rights and duties in the enterprise—The revolutionary objectives of the Four-Year Plan—Our oil industry—Electric energy is indispensable—How does our Communal People's Assembly work?—Let us join in the renascence of our national culture —etc. More immediately vocational questions were also dealt with, such as diseases of plants, irrigation and new soil management techniques.

In Iran, the project was carried out in two pilot areas (Ispahan and Dezful) and affected nearly 100,000 peasants, artisans, workers, miners, and especially women. One of the programmes concerned domestic economy. This latter sector dealt with hygiene, health, nutrition and, in particular, family planning. Just as in Algeria, there was a very high percentage of drop out (about 60 per cent) in spite of the use of modern methods and teaching aids, and in spite of an urgent demand for literacy on the part of the population.

The Experimental World Literacy Programme—a failure?

The very critical analysis of the pilot experiments in the EWLP, which was published by Unesco and UNDP, might lead one to think, at first glance, that the whole enterprise was a failure. Nothing could be more mistaken.

Thanks to these experiments and their systematic evaluation, we now know the conditions which have to be met if a literacy project is to succeed. We know the critical points which can cause the best intentioned projects to fail. Methods have been tested. Today, in short, we know much better than we did ten years ago how to go about making a success of a literacy campaign.

capable of acting upon the world, of transforming it, and of defining the aims of an authentic human development. It should open the way to a mastery of techniques and human relations. Literacy is not an end in itself. It is a fundamental human right.

It is true that all social structures give rise to the type of education which can maintain and reproduce them, and that the purposes of education are subordinated to the purposes of the dominant groups; but it would be incorrect to conclude that there is nothing to be done within the existing system.

Literacy, like education in general, is not the driving force of historical change. It is not the only means of liberation but it is an essential instrument for all social change.

Literacy work, like education in general, is a political act. . . .

Consequently, there are economic, social, political and administrative structures that favour the accomplishment of literacy projects, others that hinder them.

The most favourable structures would be:

— Those that, from the political point of view, tend to bring about the effective participation of every citizen in decision-making at all levels of social life: in economics, politics and culture.

— Those that, from the economic point of view, aim at an endogenous and harmonious development of society, and not at blind and dependent growth.

— Those that, from the social point of view, do not result in making education a class privilege and a means of reproducing established hierarchies and orders.

— Those that, from the professional point of view, provide communities with genuine control over the technologies they wish to use.

— Those that, from the institutional point of view, favour a concerted approach and permanent co-operation among the authorities responsible for basic services (agriculture, welfare, health, family planning, etc.).

Continued on page 72

In spite of this, the results of the EWLP caused some disappointment. In the first place, it did not lead to any major adult literacy campaigns. Secondly, it did not convincingly reveal what connexions might exist between functional literacy and economic and social development, which had been one of the main objectives of the programme.

What lessons can be learned from the EWLP? First, we must realize that the problems of adult literacy are much more complex than was originally thought. The second is one of paramount importance: winning the battle of literacy is primarily a question of political will. History, moreover, has already proved this. The industrialized countries of Western Europe and America have fought this battle by introducing compulsory education and they have won it. The USSR made gigantic efforts after the revolution and gained a spectacular success. China, where 80 per cent of all adults were illiterate before its great campaign, has conquered illiteracy, as has also, more recently, Cuba. Other countries, such as Algeria and the United Republic of Tanzania, seem to be on the way to success.

Obviously, some countries where EWLP pilot projects were carried out were partly disappointed in them; they would have preferred large-scale, much more spectacular campaigns than these almost isolated experiments. What the governments were hoping for above all was action, whereas the international organizations wished to evaluate what might seem to be only highly sophisticated experiments. In the eyes of the governments concerned, all that experimentation contributed very little to the urgent search for a solution of the problem of illiteracy in their respective countries.

Political will and choice

Political will is undoubtedly the primary prerequisite for the success of a literacy campaign. However, the necessary resources must also be available.

At first glance, it does not seem that adult literacy should cost very much. In spite of the fact that it is difficult to make any exact comparison of the figures produced by the EWLP experiments, it can be stated that it is possible to teach an adult to read and write for a sum of $50 to $100. Is this cheap? It is an enormous sum in a country where the annual per capita income is less than $100.

In the battle against illiteracy, children's schooling plays a very important, if not decisive, part. Universal school attendance is the

Experience has shown that literacy can bring about the alienation of the individual by integrating him in an order established without his consent. It can integrate him, without his participation, in a foreign development model or, on the contrary, help to expand his critical awareness and creative imagination, thereby enabling every man to participate, as a responsible agent, in all the decisions affecting his destiny.

The success of literacy efforts is closely connected with national political will. Ways exist of attaining the objectives which result from the definition of literacy on which the Symposium based its work.

The ways and means of literacy activities should be founded on the specific characteristics of the environment, personality and identity of each people. True education must be rooted in the culture and civilization of each people, aware of its unique contribution to universal culture and open to a fertile dialogue with other civilizations.

Literacy is effective to the extent that the people to whom it is addressed, in particular women and the least privileged groups (such as migrant workers), feel the need for it in order to meet their most essential requirements, in particular the need to take part in the decisions of the community to which they belong.

Literacy is therefore inseparable from participation, which is at once its purpose and its condition. The illiterate should not be the object but the subject of the process whereby he becomes literate. A far-reaching mobilization of human resources implies the commitment of literacy students and teachers alike. The latter should not form a specialized and permanent professional body, but should be recruited as close as possible to the masses undergoing literacy training and should belong to the same or to a related social and professional group in order to make dialogue easier.

The effectiveness of this mobilization will be increased if greater respect is paid to the initiative of the populations concerned and to consultation with them, instead of abiding by bureaucratic decisions imposed from outside and above. The motivation of those involved will be stronger if each

Continued on page 74

surest means to achieve, after a few decades, the desired objective.[1] However, in many countries, due to the lack of resources, the achievement of universal school education still lies in the relatively remote future.

In view of the high rates of drop out in the literacy courses (approximately one out of every two adults in the EWLP experiments), it would be futile to admit that this plague can be permanently eliminated by teaching adults to read and write. As long as a government does not have the means to put all its children in school, it will have to make the following choice: which is more worthwhile, to send another child to school or to teach an adult to read and write? Or then it will try to combine school education with out-of-school education; however, no ideal and really effective solution for this highly complex problem has yet been found.

The great majority of countries are now opting for school education. As is probably the case everywhere in the world, the demand for school education is more insistent than the demand for adult education. One of the only statesmen who has a different point of view on this subject seems to be Julius Nyerere, President of the United Republic of Tanzania, who said in 1967: 'We must first teach the adults. It will be five, ten or even twenty years before our children have any effect on our economic development.'

The EWLP was unable to produce any clear proof of the existence of a direct causality between literacy and development. The economic profitability of adult literacy has not yet been proved. However, it seems obvious that a literacy rate of 30 to 50 per cent is a necessary, though hardly sufficient, condition for economic growth.

There is still another aspect to consider. Literacy is meaningless without the creation of an infrastructure to ensure the supply of reading matter: newspapers, books, etc. It is believed that more than 60 per cent of adults who have known how to read and write at one time, relapse into illiteracy every year because of the lack of light reading matter. Literacy campaigns—like school education—cannot be limited to learning to read and write. A literacy campaign, therefore, also means obtaining paper, constructing printing presses, establishing publishing houses, starting up distribution networks, creating libraries

---

1. In 1965, the International Conference on Public Education rightly said: 'Illiteracy must be eliminated at its source if it is to be completely abolished, and all children must therefore be enrolled at school as soon as possible' (Recommendation no. 58).

community is itself given the opportunity of carrying out the literacy project.

The methods and material means should be diversified, flexible and suited to the environment and needs of the new literates, as opposed to a uniform and rigid model.

Literacy work of this kind would constitute the first stage of basic education designed to bring about the individual development of men and women through continuing training and to improve the environment as a whole. It would permit the development of non-formal education for the benefit of all those who are excluded by the present system or are unable to take advantage of it. Finally, it will imply a radical reform of the structures of the education system as a whole.

The importance of audio-visual aids for literacy was fully recognized. However attempts to take over these aids on grounds of technical necessity by economic or political forces beyond the control of the peoples concerned, and their use as instruments of cultural colonization, should be rejected.... Programmes should be drawn up in consultation with those concerned, through an exchange of information on significant experiences.

Literacy work should encourage the participants to acquire a wide range of communication skills.

The accomplishment of these tasks calls for a priority claim on national and local financial and human resources. In certain situations, the appeal of countries for complementary international financial co-operation supplied, *inter alia*, by international and regional institutions, may be justified in the light of special needs, particularly with regard to equipment and to the training of personnel. The use of complicated equipment which the recipient community could not fully control should not be encouraged....

Literacy work is of world-wide concern, requiring that ideological, geographical and economic distinctions be transcended.

While its primary field of operation is in the Third World, the new international order gives it a universal dimension, through which the concrete solidarity of nations and the common destiny of man must find expression.

and bookstores. In recent years, however, thanks partly to help by Unesco, rural newspapers have been founded for the benefit of persons who have just learned to read in such countries as Congo, Mali, Niger, Togo and the United Republic of Tanzania.

The task is an enormous one, since these infrastructures have to be created from the ground up, particularly in rural areas with a low population density where transport facilities are often inadequate. It would certainly be unfair to reproach poor countries for hesitating to undertake literacy campaigns on a large scale.

There are still other important lessons to be learned from the experience of the last few years.

Literacy cannot be considered as a project independent of the development process. It is one of the factors of it. For this reason, it is absolutely necessary that literacy projects be made an integral part of over-all development plans. They must be part of a single strategy. Most of the failures and disappointments connected with literacy campaigns tend to prove the correctness of this argument.

However necessary the political will of governments may be in eliminating illiteracy, any effort in this field will be futile unless it is supported at the base, i.e. by a strong motivation among the population. To carry out a major literacy campaign successfully would seem to call for an especially dynamic effort. Some authors even think that major literacy campaigns cannot succeed unless they are part of a revolutionary process.[1] They believe that only such a process is capable of releasing the necessary forces to accomplish a task of this magnitude.

It seems certain that a literacy campaign has no chance of success unless it is based on the total participation of the population concerned. In that case the problem of the necessary resources will change completely. 'Experience has shown that if a community is highly motivated, it can find the means for financing the education it requires' [119p, p. 81]. Concerning this subject, an appeal launched by Ho Chi Minh in 1954 says the following:

In order to safeguard our independence and to make our country strong and prosperous, each Vietnamese citizen should know his rights and his duties, and he should be capable of contributing to the work of national

---

1. 'Recent history has shown that, up to now, revolutionary régimes have been the only ones capable of organizing successful mass literacy campaigns', as Professor Lê Thank Khôi recently wrote in an article published in the review *Prospects* [119p, p. 111].

construction. Above all, everyone should be able to read and write. Those who already know how to read and write should pass their knowledge on to the others. The illiterate should make every effort to learn. Husbands should teach their wives; older brothers and sisters should teach their younger brothers and sisters; children should teach their parents; the master of the house should teach those living beneath his roof [119p, p. 112].

In Somalia, where the revolutionary government inaugurated a national literacy campaign on 8 March 1973, all educated Somalis were appointed teachers and all illiterate persons became students. The slogan was: 'If you know, teach ! If you don't know, learn !' [21e].

Experiments now under way

In 1970, 33.6 per cent of the Brazilian population of more than 15 years of age, i.e. 18 million adults, were illiterate and, therefore, under the Brazilian constitution, did not have the right to vote or to be elected to public office. The Brazilian Literacy Movement (Mobral), which was created by the Government for the speedy and complete eradication of illiteracy throughout the country, began to function in 1970 [156; 90]. During the first five years of its existence, Mobral, thanks to the Government's unstinting support, succeeded in teaching more than 8 million persons to read and write, thus reducing the illiteracy rate to 18.7 per cent. To achieve this result, Mobral mobilized the 3,963 communes of the country, established 1,200,000 literacy centres and distributed 100 million copies of instructional materials. Mobral, therefore, opted for a mass strategy to which it adapted all the elements involved: organizations, instructional materials, the training of personnel, a sub-system of over-all supervision, etc. To carry out this strategy, it is resorting more and more to such highly effective techniques as radio, television and the automatic data processing of class years. Since it is convinced that the degree of literacy acquired after only five or six months of study does not provide a sufficient stock of knowledge for the man of today, Mobral is organizing programmes of integrated education and community and cultural development. In Brazilian education as a whole, these constitute the germ of an integrated system of adult education which will conform to the concept of lifelong education. The only things which do not seem to have been entirely solved in this vast campaign are the problems of post-literacy, such as supplying sufficient reading matter which is adapted to the real needs of newly literate persons and understandable to all of them, so as to prevent them from relapsing into illiteracy.

As appears from, *inter alia*, the national reports presented at the thirty-fifth session of the International Conference on Education, a number of other Latin American countries have launched literacy campaigns. This is the case, for example, in Bolivia, Colombia, the Dominican Republic, Mexico, Peru, Venezuela, etc. It is characteristic of this part of the world that radio is a strong buttress of these projects almost everywhere.

In India, the Government's campaign against illiteracy has been going on since 1957. In an initial phase, thanks to the work of the Directorate of Non-formal (Adult) Education of the Federal Ministry of Education and Social Affairs, the Government became aware of the importance of adult literacy for national development. During the 1950s, the prevailing concept was that of social education as an integral part of community development. During the 1960s, emphasis was placed on the functionality linking literacy to specific objectives of development. A project linking literacy to rural promotion and agricultural production was launched for a homogeneous group of farmers working on varieties of high-yield crops and living in the area where the 'Green Revolution' was taking place. During the 1970s, the concept of literacy was broadened to include communication skills on a larger scale of human activities and adapted to environmental needs, the emphasis being placed on the socio-cultural aspects. Priority was then given to young people between 15 and 25 years of age. In 1975, more than 300,000 adults benefited from the national programmes of functional literacy for farmers and the programmes of non-formal education for young people between 15 and 25. These programmes extend all over the country and are distributed among 10,000 centres. Moreover, 200,000 adults have benefited by the programmes organized by the different States, local organizations and voluntary agencies, while another 100,000, who live in urban and industrial areas, are engaged in studies based on programmes for illiterates or semi-illiterates. A vast programme has beeen carried out for the preparation of miscellaneous instructional materials for functional literacy projects, of which there are approximately 100 different kinds.

Pakistan has drawn up a very ambitious plan aimed at teaching more than 6 million adults to read and write during the period 1975-80.[1] This programme is combined with a considerable strengthening of formal and non-formal education for young people. About

1. See Pakistan's report to the thirty-fifth session of the International Conference on Education.

280,000 literacy centres should be created between now and 1980. In addition, it is planned to build a large number of miscellaneous vocational schools and youth centres. The People's Open University, which has already been mentioned (see p. 62) is expected to play an important part in this campaign.

On the occasion of the eleventh International Literacy Day (8 September 1976), His Imperial Highness the Shahinshah of Iran delivered a message announcing the launching of a new campaign against illiteracy.

In organizing this campaign, very careful attention will have to be paid to its primordial aspects on the national level; we must therefore pay particular heed to the children, all of whom should benefit by education, to those villages where illiteracy is most common, and to the working classes. All organizations must offer their services to this campaign and devote all their resources to it. Of course, the private sector must not remain inactive, for this problem affects the entire nation.

Most of the Arab countries have stated their desire to eliminate illiteracy. The majority of them have enacted laws concerning literacy (Egypt, Iraq, the Libyan Arab Jamahiriya, Oman, Saudi Arabia, Sudan, the Syrian Arab Republic, Tunisia, Yemen and Democratic Yemen) or are in the process of preparing them. In some of these texts, literacy is compulsory. Side by side with pilot and selective projects, some countries in this area are beginning to plan the total elimination of illiteracy and have set a deadline for this objective (five to ten years for Iraq, ten years for Jordan and Sudan, fifteen years for Egypt, twenty years for Saudi Arabia).

On the occasion of a national conference held at the highest level in Baghdad in May 1976, Iraq drew up its strategy for a literacy campaign aimed at the whole population. This far-reaching plan provides for an approach to the problem which uses the most modern concepts in this field and places particular emphasis on the cultural and social dimensions of literacy. This strategy calls for universal and compulsory primary education and the integration of the education system as a whole from the point of view of lifelong education.

Among the African countries which are making special efforts to eliminate illiteracy is the Somali Democratic Republic, where very original projects have been carried out. We might mention, for example, the action taken by the Somali Women's Organization. From 1974 to 1975, this organization took an active part in the rural development campaign, which included literacy programmes, as well as health and veterinary education. Thanks to this campaign, more than 400,000 women have been taught to read and write. Through their organization, the women of Somalia have already taught an elementary knowledge of reading, writing and arithmetic to 1,200,000 persons. They have also helped to build schools where children can be educated at the same time as their mothers.

In 1974, the Chairman of the Somali National Committee launched a major literacy campaign. From July of that year, all the schools in the country closed for one year to make it possible to implement this programme. The teachers and students were sent to rural areas to teach the peasants to read and write.

Incidentally, illiteracy is not a phenomenon which is peculiar to developing countries. A proof of this is that the BBC in London recently launched, with great success, a literacy progamme in the United Kingdom.

Goals of adult literacy

For several years, people have begun to reflect seriously on the goals of literacy. The simple statement that the acquisition of a minimum amount of knowledge and access to the world of today is a fundamental human right had to be more carefully qualified, more sharply defined, in order to bring out its underlying significance. There was a danger that the concept of functional literacy might confine the problem of illiteracy to a context that was too narrowly economic. For this reason, the notion of functional literacy in Peru, for example, was replaced by that of integral literacy. This new awareness of the meaning of literacy is to be found in the reorientation of the whole philosophy of development, in which it is beginning to be realized that development is not only an economic problem but also a problem of social justice, and that its essential dimension is of a cultural nature. The subject and goal of development is man himself!

For this reason, the question arises whether literacy should be limited to learning such techniques as reading, writing, elementary arithmetic and a few vocational ideas, with a view to increasing economic productivity?

Recent replies given to this kind of question all tend towards a considerable expansion of the dimensions of literacy campaigns. In the report of the International Commission on the Development of Education, *Learning to be*, we read the following on this subject:

The aim [of the campaign against illiteracy] is not simply to enable an illiterate person to decipher words in a textbook but to become better integrated into his environment, to have a better grasp of real life, to enhance his personal dignity, to have access to sources of knowledge which he personally may find useful, to acquire the know-how and the techniques he needs in order to lead a better life [54, p. 39].

At the Persepolis Symposium, where M. Rahnema had asked the question: 'Is the purpose of literacy to read the words or the world ?', all these problems were discussed at length [119p]. From the results of this very important and significant event, it is clearly evident that any literacy campaign today is considered to be a process aimed at developing every individual as a member of his society. The acquisition of reading and writing techniques is considered almost secondary, as a mere vehicle or by-product.

For illiteracy is only one symptom of a particularly precarious human condition, and it is the root of the evils that should be attacked.

Who are the ones who make up the majority of illiterates ? It is primarily the poorest of the poor. Especially peasants in underdeveloped areas, living far from cities. The elderly. Those who have no means of changing their living conditions. Those caught up in the vicious circle of poverty-ignorance-malnutrition-lethargy-poverty, who live without any hope of a better life, without any hope of freedom.

The notion of the 'functionality' of literacy therefore takes on a profound meaning and much broader dimensions. And the campaign against illiteracy becomes an eminently political question.[1] From this point of view, literacy is considered to be an essential facet of any process of democratization in the developing countries. Perhaps this is one of the reasons why large-scale literacy campaigns are so slow in reaching many countries where social injustices are as great as those which characterize the relations between developed countries and countries of the Third World.

---

1. M. RAHNEMA says the following on this subject: 'Literacy, as conscientization, is not neutral—like education—it transcends the sheer learning of a technical skill; it has a political content, in the widest meaning of the word. ... As such, its success depends upon the political will of a society to transform its structure, to create a new conception of man and re-define the nature of the relationships among men' [119p, p. 75]. A.E. LIZARZABURU also says: 'It is possible to eliminate illiteracy only within the framework of a global strategy aimed at bringing about a revolutionary transformation in the social structure' [119p, p. 103].

Since illiteracy can no longer be considered a marginal problem concerning marginal people, governments and the international community are beginning to realize that literacy should be conceived of as a genuine educational process in the most general sense of the word. What is involved is an essential aspect, and, for countries with a high rate of illiteracy, the most urgent aspect of adult education. What is involved, consequently, is a process which constitutes a priority element in lifelong education. This is why literacy raises all the fundamental problems raised by any educational activity. It is also why, in countries where illiteracy is rampant, the aspect of literacy will have to be integrated in any over-all educational reform.

In spite of all, let us end on an optimistic note: illiteracy will continue to persist for many decades, but the day will come when this plague will disappear. And it is probably the only educational problem which one day will be definitely solved.

Chapter Three

The democratization
of education

The democratization of education is a subject of priority concern for every country in the world and for all those who deal with educational questions. It is a leitmotif which can be found again and again in most of the innumerable speeches and publications on education. Sometimes as a fashionable political or idealistic slogan, at other times as a serious preoccupation and the object of profound analyses, the democratization of education is an inexhaustible subject and a concept which covers practically all educational problems. It is difficult, in fact, to find one question in the field of education which does not contain, in one way or another, some aspect of 'democratization'.

Taken in its deeper sense, the democratization of education reflects the aspirations of mankind to a more just world, where human rights would be fully guaranteed to all.

In the effort to carry out this democratization, it has been realized that it could not be reduced to the simple notion, for example, of equality of opportunity or to non-discrimination in obtaining access to schools. In recent years, the concept of the democratization of education has been enriched by precise meanings. To become a reality, it calls for concrete measures of very different kinds.

EQUALITY OF OPPORTUNITY
AND THE STRUGGLE AGAINST DISCRIMINATION

A discussion of equality of opportunity may cover a number of different aspects. It can refer to equality within a given society, especially within a State—or equality of opportunity on a much more general scale, i.e. at the international level. In this chapter, we shall limit ourselves to the national level, as international problems are dealt with mainly in the section on education and development (p. 129-41). 'Equality of opportunity' may also mean equality of opportunity 'in living' or equality of opportunity 'in education'. These two conceptions, which are different although interdependent, are very often confused. We shall concentrate almost exclusively on the second one.

Outwardly, the problem of equality of opportunity in education is relatively simple. In some countries, there are flagrant cases of discrimination in education, such as those concerning girls, special racial groups or minorities. Certain underprivileged groups, such as the children of migrant workers or the handicapped, suffer from a lack of education. In addition, statistics show that, to a certain extent, success in school depends on the milieu to which the pupil belongs. The traditional school system favours the privileged social circles. In order to remedy this situation, which is contrary to the principles of human rights and social justice, it is necessary to change the school structures or, better still, the education systems as a whole, with a view to putting an end to discrimination and the negative effects of social environments. Henri Janne sums it up as follows: 'The principle of equality of opportunity means that any natural, economic, social or cultural inferiority should be compensated as far as possible by the educative system itself' [131, p. xiii], a theory which is generally accepted today.

During the last few decades, a number of measures aimed at these objectives have been developed and applied in many countries. They conform to a democratic ideal, the ideal of all the great teachers, from Comenius and Pestalozzi to those of our own time. In very recent years, however, we have begun to realize that measures aimed at guaranteeing equality of opportunity to everybody have not always given the desired results. Questions and criticisms are heard more and more often and doubts continue to grow. The problem seems more complex than we had thought, especially if we enlarge it to include that of the equality of opportunity in life.

The obstacles

In the countries of the Third World where, due to lack of resources, the education systems are not sufficiently developed to permit all children to go to school, we can still find the worst of all inequalities: that which creates two classes of citizens, the educated and the illiterate. The school then becomes a decisive factor in creating inequalities by educating élites which, by the force of circumstances, are going to become dominant minorities. Incidentally, this is one of the reasons why, in the nineteenth century, the founders of democracies insisted so strongly on the introduction of compulsory education for all.

Within the countries themselves, differences in the level of development, which are often very pronounced between different areas—especially between urban and rural areas—are a serious factor in the inequality of opportunity.[1]

The influence of the environment already begins in the prenatal stage. Today it is well known that the mother's state of health and way of life, as well as the nutritional condition of the newborn baby later on, can influence the intelligence and character of the child. The family surroundings condition a child's attitudes in many ways. They may awaken his curiosity, stimulate him and above all teach him to express himself, or, on the contrary, inhibit his full development. The school of today has a very marked tendency to favour oral expression, and ease of expression is in direct ratio to the socio-cultural environment in which the child is brought up. Moreover, in developing countries the teaching is very often in a different language than that spoken by the parents, especially if the latter do not belong to the upper social strata. This handicap is also very often found among the children of migrant workers. The way in which the mother influences the child, follows his development and helps him to do his lessons is equally important. A child who can work quietly at home will be more at ease than one who lives in one room surrounded by many brothers and sisters. However, besides the environment of the parents and the groups of young people in which the child is living, the school environment itself is, among so many others, a decisive factor for success or failure in the school. Lastly, there is the motivation for studies, and above all for continuing studies, which is normally much stronger in comfortable and educated circles than in poor and ignorant families. This motivation is often decisive. We might add that it is a factor which is particularly responsible for the inequality of opportunity in education among girls. Another argument in this debate runs as follows: the evaluation procedures in school systems are designed to conform to the value systems of specific and dominant social groups. It is therefore only natural that children from these groups should be more successful than those who belong to other social strata.

---

1. See section in Chapter Four, 'Education in the rural world' (p. 152-4).

The question of determining to what extent hereditary factors are responsible for the failure of efforts to equalize opportunity in education has often given rise to passionate discussions. It may be stated that, on the basis of large-scale research, there has for several years been a growing tendency to grant more weight to heredity and to question those theories which state that the main responsibility for inequalities in education is due to differences between socio-cultural environments.

Measures

Identical measures to reduce inequalitites in education, and especially to relieve socio-cultural handicaps, have been taken in all countries which have reformed their education system along the lines of greater democratization. We shall review them briefly.

Since the end of the 1960s, and especially in Europe, public opinion and public authorities have been paying increasing attention to pre-school education. On the basis of the results of scientific research carried out for the most part in the United States—and in Switzerland by Jean Piaget—it is acknowledged today that: 'early childhood is the vital period for all learning, talent forming and personality development' [33, p. 80]. For this reason, pre-school education seems to be the ideal means of making up for the deficiencies and unfavourable influences of underprivileged environments. This compensatory role of pre-school educational establishments has been brought into even stronger relief by the emancipation of women, with the result that an increasing number of mothers are now working outside the home.[1]

Whereas in the large majority of African and Asian countries, formal *pre-school education* is, for obvious reasons, non-existent and considered a luxury,[2] its importance is being recognized more and more in the countries of Latin America. In this area, the proportion of pre-school education has increased by 9.6 per cent, while primary education has expanded by only 4.1 per cent. For several years in these countries, educational establishments have not only been found

---

1. In 1975, in the Federal Republic of Germany, the number of children of less than 3 years of age whose mothers were working outside the home was estimated at approximately 800,000 [33, p. 81].

2. However, in the Democratic People's Republic of Korea, one year of pre-school education was made compulsory for all children in the higher kindergarten classes (4 to 5 years) by a law enacted on 29 April 1976 at Pyongyang.

in the cities, but also in the semi-urban or even rural areas. This is the case, for example, in Argentina, Cuba, Chile, El Salvador and Peru. The industrialized countries of North America and Europe are experiencing a rapid expansion of pre-school education. As shown in Table 1, it is almost universal in some of these countries. In Poland, the school reform announced in October 1973 provides for universal pre-school education in both the cities and the countryside. The nursery school will constitute the first level of public education and will be closely linked to the educational and teaching activity of the primary school.

TABLE 1. Percentage of children attending a pre-school establishment in 1974 (based on the replies to a Unesco questionnaire).

Country	3 to 4 years	4 to 5 years	5 to 6 years	6 to 7 years
Belgium	85		98	
Brazil				20
Czechoslovakia			72	
France	50	80	75	
Federal Republic of Germany		27	33.4	
Guatemala			5.6	
Israel	35	80	95	
Japan	18	64	83	
Nicaragua				2.8
Poland	25	30	50	80
Spain	13.8	42	68	
Sweden				90
United States of America			76	

Source : Gaston MIALARET, *L'éducation prescolaire dans le monde* [89, p. 27].

It should be noted that the institutions engaged in pre-school education differ in the extreme. They vary from ordinary day-nurseries, in their various forms, to real sub-primary schools where the children learn reading, writing and arithmetic, and where, in some cases, they are even taught the first principles of modern mathematics or a second language.

Unfortunately, we have to point out a few dark spots in this over-optimistic picture. As Gaston Mialaret has already pointed out:

'there is still [a gap] in many countries between the stated goals of pre-school education and the existing situation' [89, p. 34]. Extremely divergent objectives exist side by side, and there is no co-ordination between the activities of the different categories of establishments. Moreover, very often there is little or no co-ordination between pre-school education and the teaching in the primary schools. For this reason, 'the transition from pre-school to primary education is experienced by the child as a further break, and perhaps as a cause of subsequent lack of adaptation and failure at school' [89, p. 52].

However, what is still more serious is that we have to admit that it is primarily children in the rich countries and from the middle classes who profit by pre-school education. 'So the inequitable development of pre-school education, despite the concern with social justice implicit in its goals, is yet another factor in social segregation' [89, p. 60]. Pre-school education will be unable to play its important role on behalf of the equalization of opportunity except in those places where it will be made universal or even compulsory. Such a development is not encouraged by the budgetary restrictions now existing in almost all administrations. 'The humanistic and generous efforts to establish social justice and egalitarianism in so far as school is concerned are neutralized by hard social and economic facts' [89, p. 60].

In this connexion, mention should be made of the education of the parents. But parents coming from underprivileged environments do not seem to show any special interest in this kind of activity. The impact of the parents' education on the equalization of opportunity is therefore almost non-existent.

Another means of removing children from the influences of their environment is to give them equal opportunities in education and to *prolong the duration of their schooling*, not only at the start but also at the end. This is a trend which can be observed in most developed countries. Secondary education is becoming universal. The twenty-fourth Congress of the Community Party of the Soviet Union (1971) set as its goal, in the current five-year plan, the achievement of a complete transition to compulsory secondary education. In the Federal Republic of Germany, it is thought that, by 1980, 50 per cent of all young people will graduate from secondary school. In France, it is expected that by the same time, all young people of 18 years will be enrolled in some form of full-time education [6, p. 23-4].

The extension of the length of school attendance obviously has certain limits, which probably have already been reached in some of the more advanced countries. Beyond these limits, the school will have to be replaced by other educational institutions. Recurrent education in Sweden [119o, p. 511-23] is a very promising model (see p. 54-9).

Moreover, certain countries such as New Zealand and the Netherlands have recently asked the question: should we introduce widespread compulsory secondary education when our schools, which are already open to all, are unsuccessful in retaining their students? Drop out after the compulsory period can be interpreted as a criticism of the existing schools, and therefore serves as an inducement to look for new formulas, such as the part-time education of young workers in the Netherlands.

Along with this tendency to prolong the duration of education, there is also a tendency to put off any selection as long as possible, and thus any diversification, privileged stream or specialization. The '*common cores*' extended. It is becoming increasingly less common to separate the 'élite' sections from the 'ordinary' sections, the 'humanities' from 'technology'. In many countries, we can see a widespread introduction of the model of the Anglo-Saxon 'comprehensive schools', which have been copied in the Federal Republic of Germany (*Gesamtschule*), in Sweden and recently in Finland, where all children of the same age attend courses together, without any separate branches or specialization, until the end of their compulsory schooling. Orientation or 'guidance' is becoming increasingly important, particularly in this kind of institution. Experiments are under way, in Switzerland for example, with 'unified guidance cycles' (*cycles entiers d'orientation*). An effort is being made to individualize the educational process by introducing elective subjects, so that every pupil will be assured of the complete development of all his abilities. In order to increase equality of opportunity, the practice of 'positive discrimination' is being followed, especially by devoting greater attention to the more backward pupils. Compensatory education also comes under this heading.

There are certain particularly underprivileged groups in education: the children of migrant workers; refugees; persons who are physically or mentally handicapped; marginal cases. These are very different groups, with separate and distinct problems. However, they have one trait in common: their problems have been ignored or neglected for a long time. Under the pressure of public opinion, which has been aroused by political movements or by young people with a particularly keen sense of social injustice, government authorities have, in their turn, become aware of them.

The problems of *the education of migrant workers' children* are recognized as entitled to priority throughout the world (with the possible exception of the Eastern European States), both by countries which export manpower and the host countries which receive these workers and their families. International or regional organizations such as Unesco, ILO, OECD, the Council of Europe, the European Economic Community, etc., have all placed this question on their agendas.

In November 1974, an Ad Hoc Conference of European Ministers of Education on the Education of Migrants was held at Strasbourg under the auspices of the Council of Europe.

Besides the difficulties created by socio-cultural uprooting in general, the greatest handicap experienced by migrant workers and their families is the one of language. In the host countries, children can often be found speaking different languages in the same class. It is easy to imagine the problems which arise in such a case and which may continue to exist in spite of the organization of reception, transitional, adjustment or opportunity classes, language courses, supervised studies, etc. Another special problem is that of the mother tongue and the original culture, which ought not to be lost, particularly in view of a possible return to the country of origin. One trend became very clearly evident during the Conference of European Ministers, as well as in other gatherings: the children of migrant workers must be treated on a footing of strict equality with the children of the host country, in respect of both their rights and their obligations; and above all they must not be segregated in special classes or other educational ghettos, except possibly for a period of adjustment to enable them to learn the language of the country of immigration as quickly as possible.

At the beginning of 1976, the Ministers of Education of the African States, meeting at Lagos, adopted a resolution concerning *the education of the handicapped*.[1] This is a remarkable fact. In all parts of the

---

1. The text of this resolution is as follows:

   'The Conference,

   Considering that each individual has the right to a minimum of education which will enable him to realize his potential and contribute to the economic, social and cultural development of the nation to which he belongs,

world there is an awareness of the problems raised by special education, including countries which are still carrying on a bitter and almost
desperate battle to introduce universal school attendance.[1]

It is perhaps premature to try to single out any general trends in
the development of special education at this time. They are making
only a tentative appearance, but they all seem to be moving in a
direction similar to the one we have noted elsewhere in this chapter.
The pre-school phase is recognized as being a particularly important
phase for preventing a handicap from becoming worse and, if possible,
for integrating young handicapped persons in the school and forestall-
ing subsequent scholastic failures. Sweden has come out with a new
conception of the problem by saying that 'pupils who experience difficulties of varying types and importance in their schooling as the
result of environmental or heriditary factors and physical or mental
disorders' [147, p. 22] (the Swedes avoid using the term 'handicapped'),
should be integrated as closely as possible in regular schools, either
individually in regular classes or at least by groups, with the help of
special classes. That is a conception, already followed in Japan and
elsewhere, which is opposed to the isolation of the handicapped,
to their segregation, and which conforms perfectly to the measures
aimed at equalizing opportunity in education by abolishing the existence of different categories of pupils according to different kinds or
branches of education. In a system of this kind, a certain individualization of education, 'guidance' and 'educational assistance', are important factors. In Cuba and elsewhere, 'schools for parents' have been
specially established, where reports and courses are organized on
special education and the various problems of handicapped persons.

In recent years, the inequality of the sexes and *discrimination against
girls* in education have been very widely discussed, especially during
International Women's Year (1975).[2] The facts of the problem are

---

Recommends:
1. that efforts be made by African Member States to identify handicapped
   youths in the society, and to set up suitable educational facilities for these
   handicapped children;
2. that training facilities be established on African soil for teachers of handicapped children' [21k, p. 39].

1. Four case studies of different areas are contained in the Unesco publication,
   Case studies in special education: Cuba, Japan, Kenya, Sweden [147].
2. See, for example: Unesco, *Women, education and equality: a decade of experiment* [153].

therefore well known. Unfortunately, in a large majority of countries, the question is far from a solution. This is proved irrefutably by the statistics on education. However, it is equally undeniable that progress is being made. Almost everywhere where this problem still persists, action is being taken or is proposed to give girls the same opportunities as boys. In accordance with the general trend towards the abolition of all forms of educational segregation, coeducation is gaining ground everywhere.

The mother's role is of paramount importance in any educational process. Equality of opportunity in education, and especially non-discrimination with regard to girls, depend to a very large extent on the mothers, on their attitude, their help, their understanding and their ability to motivate the child towards an education.

From the point of view of lifelong education, a discussion of equality of opportunity should not be limited to a single educational sector. Out-of-school education, adult education, recurrent education, all these different forms of education take on important complementary, compensatory and other functions. Having already dealt with these questions above, in another context, we shall not revert to them here.

Questions and criticisms

The developments and tendencies which we have just described are not welcomed by everybody with the same enthusiasm. They lead to questions, criticisms and disappointments. Such doubts may be based on political convictions, philosophical arguments and educational experience.

For many of those who advocate it, equality of educational opportunity is not an end in itself. It is aimed at a much greater social and political equality, at a general democratization, and often not only at a more just society but, in the last analysis, at a classless society.[1] This is a political option which is not shared by everybody.

1. 'By equality we are thinking more of the end result—the extent to which society is so constructed as to allow for a minimum of disparity in terms of power and privilege. The only concrete example of that kind is probably China, and to some extent in Tanzania...', writes Johan GALTUNG in his article *Educational growth and educational disparity* [119n, p. 324]. Moreover, in his book *Education without frontiers*, Gabriel FRAGNIERE states that 'egalitarianism in the education system is not consistent with a global society which would continue to be of an

Before any education begins, there is always an individual, born of parents having particular characteristics, in a social milieu, a cultural atmosphere and a natural environment, all of which will shape him; but nevertheless this individual has his own physique, his own character, sensibility, aptitudes, abilities, intelligence, ambitions and dreams. And all through his lifetime he will remain that same unique and irreplaceable individual. Will such an individual not find himself in conflict with an education which is too egalitarian? Especially if that individual is specially (and thus often unilaterally) gifted? Many fear that he will.

Does not egalitarianism lead to a levelling off in the quality of education and, consequently, to a compromise in favour of lower quality? Many educators seem to be convinced of this. And do we not owe to this élitism, which is so much disparaged, the great works of our cultural heritage? Some think that our troubled world needs men of an intellectual and moral level far above the average.

As it is conceived of today, the equalization of educational opportunity is very often also a cause of disappointment to those who are most anxious for far-reaching changes in society. For we must acknowledge the fact that the more we eliminate the external factors (environment, etc.), which in part determine the inequality of educational opportunity, the more we are left with genetic factors only. The equalization of opportunity emphasizes individual differences; it does not reduce them. There is a danger that the result may be a pure 'meritocracy', in which the 'best' will constitute the ruling class. After all, is it not easier to endure a mediocre and even miserable lot if you can blame it on injustices of one kind or another and do not have to admit that it was your own failings alone which were responsible? [1]

We shall have to return later to this difficult discussion of the complex relations between education and society.

---

essentially hierarchic nature, where power, income and culture would continue to be shared unequally. Educational policy cannot be of a different nature than general policy. The development of systems of education cannot be too much out of step with the means of production' [56].

1. 'A meritocratic school system... will tend towards even greater inhumanity than traditional systems of unequal opportunity because of the ineluctable character of its seemingly objective measuring instruments', writes W. MITTMER in *School systems and inequality of opportunity* [25, p. 9]. See also on this question J. BENGTSSON, et al., *Does education have a future?* [6].

ACCESS TO EDUCATION,
ESPECIALLY HIGHER EDUCATION

The degree of democratization of an education system, or the equality
of opportunity offered by this system, can be measured, at least in
part, by the rates of access to the different levels of education.
However, equality of access to education is not the same thing as
equality of opportunity in education. As Johan Galtung has said:
'equality of opportunity is simply equal opportunity for competition
into an unequal society' [119n, p. 324]. He says further:

> Educational inequality is not the same as *inequality of educational
> opportunity* either. The latter refers to the *starting condition:* is the system
> made in such a way that everybody has the same chance of getting launched
> on equally good educational ladders, *or* is it made in such a way that the
> system tends to discriminate against some by denying them access, or giving
> them access only to poorer parts of the total system? Clearly, even in a
> system where everybody starts under exactly the same condition, they may
> still end up differently, and if they do so the system will produce educational
> inequality (as herein defined) [59, p. 1].

A few figures

The question of access to education is therefore in part—but only in
part—quantifiable. There are three graphs which illustrate inequalities
in access to education in different parts of the world.[1] Incidentally,
they give a rather over-optimistic picture, as do almost all official
statistics in the field of education, and especially those concerning the
Third World.

Diagram 3 illustrates total school enrolments and their increase for
each level of education, by sex and by region. One should take note of

1. All these data come from Unesco's Office of Statistics (see especially *A summary
   statistical review of education in the world, 1960-1972* [73d] from which some
   conclusions have been taken verbatim). The areas are defined as follows:
   Africa covers the entire African continent, including the Arab States of Africa.
   North America covers the United States, Canada, Bermuda, Greenland and
   St. Pierre and Miquelon. Latin America covers the South American continent,
   Central America, Mexico and the Caribbean. Asia covers the entire Asian
   region, including the Arab States of Asia. Europe includes the USSR. Oceania
   covers Australia, New Zealand and the surrounding islands. The Arab States
   as a separate grouping is presented, but they are already included partly under
   Africa and partly under Asia.

DIAGRAM 3. Total enrolment (in millions) for each level of education, by sex and area, 1960-72.

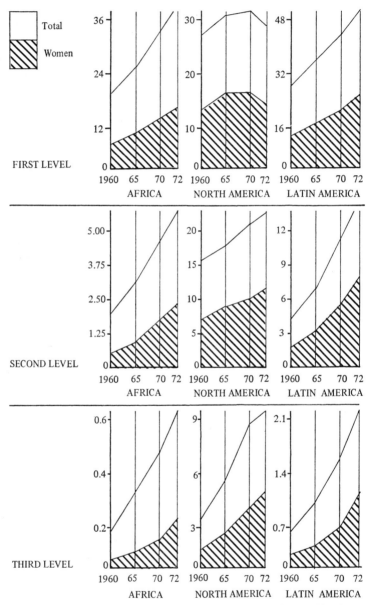

1. Not including the People's Republic of China, the Democratic People's Republic of Korea and the Socialist Republic of Viet-Nam.

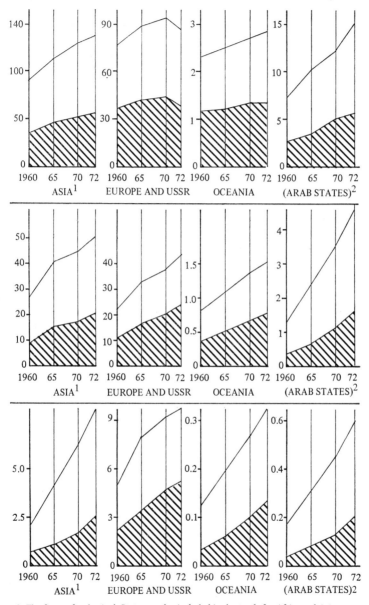

2. The figures for the Arab States are also included in the totals for Africa and Asia.

the fact that the graphs are not all drawn to the same scale. The total number of pupils and students in all three levels is about 740 million for the whole world,[1] which is almost equivalent to the number of illiterate adults estimated at about 800 million at the moment.

The high rates of increase (more than 5 per cent annually) registered between 1960 and 1965 have not been maintained, and total enrolment is now increasing by less than 3 per cent annually.[2] In fact, the over-all rate of increase is diminishing regularly. This is most pronounced in Africa, Latin America and the Arab States; in Asia it has not ceased to decline.

Although this increase is found mainly at the level of first-level education (nearly 108 million children), the relative increase has been highest in second and third-level education—5.4 and 8.2 per cent respectively for the entire period in question. In all areas, enrolment in secondary education has increased faster than in primary education, and enrolment in higher education has increased even more rapidly. The greatest increase, in fact, is found in Africa, in the third level (15.5 per cent for the period 1960-72). But it should not be forgotten that this increase starts from an extremely low level, which is clearly apparent as soon as one compares Diagram 3 with the two following ones. It would seem, therefore, that the most serious discrimination is always practised at the threshold of the first level, whereas those who have succeeded in entering the system have a better chance of gaining admission to the higher levels.

In most areas, the percentage of girls in the first and second levels has become more or less stabilized, and in North America, Europe, the USSR and Latin America both sexes now seem to be equal at these levels. The percentage of girls is lowest in higher education, although it has increased everywhere. At the present time, the lowest percentages (25 per cent) are found in Africa and in the Arab States, and the highest in North America, Europe and the USSR (43 per cent).

Diagram 4 shows the increase, by area, in rates of school attendance from 1960 to 1973 in three age groups. For the world as a whole, the rate of school attendance for children of 6 to 11 years of age increased

1. The exact figures for China, the Democratic People's Republic of Korea and the Socialist Republic of Viet-Nam are not known. However, an estimate is included in our over-all figures.
2. The growth rate of the world population of children aged 0-4 is now about 3 per cent; it is therefore slightly higher than the growth rate of school enrolment. If the trend of school enrolment rates is always on the increase, this is due more to the decline in infant mortality than to the expansion of education systems.

DIAGRAM 4. Rate of school attendance in three age groups, by area, 1960-75.

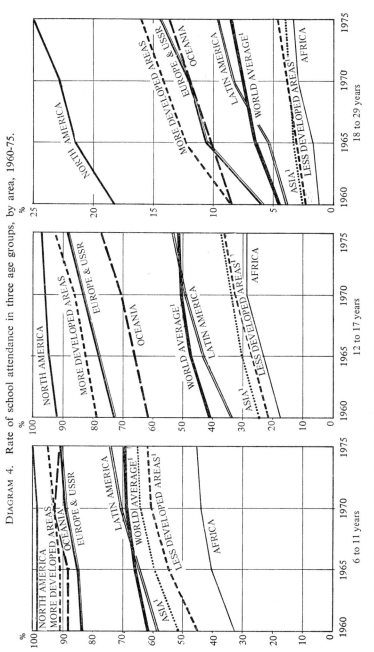

1. Not including the People's Republic of China, the Democratic People's Republic of Korea and the Socialist Republic of Viet-Nam.

from 60 per cent in 1960 to 70 per cent in 1970. This over-all figure conceals some important disparities between areas: in 1970, the rate amounted to 44 per cent in Africa and 99 per cent in North America, while all the other areas were between those two extremes, Asia being, after Africa, the area where the rate of school attendance was lowest (65 per cent). These disparities are more marked in the case of the older pupils and students. The situation of girls in relation to boys is similar to that found for school enrolment, as there was no appreciable discrimination—always according to official figures— except in a few areas and for the 18-29 age group.

Diagram 5 again shows the efforts made between 1960 and 1972, as well as the wide disparities existing between different areas. Whereas in North America, pupils in the second and third levels are more numerous, taken together, than those in the first level, in Africa, only 1.4 per cent of all pupils are enrolled in the third level. This diagram only shows the young people who are in school; those who do not attend any school—in some areas the majority !—are not included.

DIAGRAM 5. Distribution of pupils by level of education in the different regions of the world (percentage).

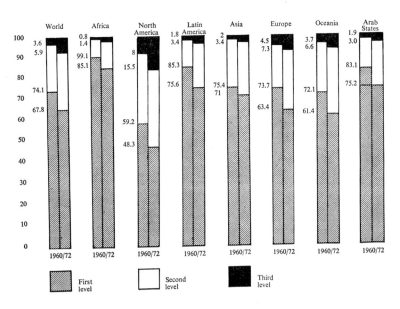

It is obvious that access to education depends on the resources which a society is able to invest in its education system. The expansion of education systems favours access to education, but not automatically equality. If the schools grow bigger and throw their doors wide open, more pupils will be able to enter—but that will not determine what happens inside. It is possible that those who enter school will find an unjust system and more or less arbitrary selections waiting for them.

Recent studies show that, in practically all the present education systems, the increased extension and efficiency of these systems seem to create greater disparities. A study made by Johan Galtung, Christian Beck and Johannes Jaastad for Unesco's Division of Educational Statistics reaches the following conclusion: 'Economic growth has not only been accompanied by economic inequality... but also by educational growth and educational inequality—and the latter seems at present to be increasing both within and between countries'. This result is based on an analysis of the level of education in eighty-six countries and of the distribution of education among the adult populations of those countries.[1]

DIAGRAM 6.   Distribution of levels of education in six countries.

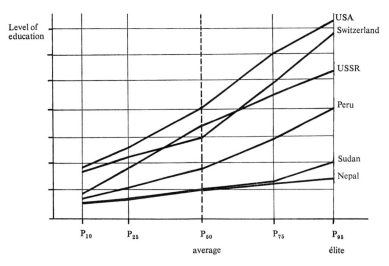

1. Johan GALTUNG, et al. *Educational growth and educational disparity* [59, p. 14-15], as well as a less technical summary of the results of this study published under the same title in the review *Prospects* [119n, p. 323-8].

Diagram 6, using the data contained in Galtung's study, gives the results of this study as shown in six characteristic examples. The scale of educational level is derived from the classification adopted by Unesco: lack of education, incomplete primary studies, complete primary studies, admission to the first stage of the second level, admission to the second stage of the second level, post-secondary studies. Point P_{50} indicates the median, i.e. the point above or below which 50 per cent of the population in question are to be found: it is their average level of education. Point P_{10} indicates the average level of the 10 per cent least educated members of that population; P_{95} the average level of the 5 per cent most educated; thus the lowest level, and the average level of the élite respectively. It will be noted that the higher the average, the greater will be the difference between the lowest level and the élite—the steeper the curve will become.

Galtung thinks he can establish a direct relation between this phenomenon and the systems of economic production (for him, the school is a factory for producing education), and more especially the division of labour (on the national as well as on the international level).

It seems to follow that it is impossible to effect any real equalization of opportunity in access to education solely by the internal transformation of the education systems, but rather that in order to attain this goal, it is necessary to make far-reaching changes in the social structures and the economic system. 'Now, however', concludes Torsten Husén, after more than twenty-five years of research on this question, 'there is a growing realization that educational reforms must be co-ordinated with social and economic reforms. Indeed, it is impossible to establish better equality of opportunity in the educational system without its being established previously or simultaneously in the over-all prevailing social system' [68, p. 164]. We shall return later to the problems of the interrelations between education and society.

In China, a process is under way aimed at unlimited equalization in all fields by a revolution of all the social, economic and, in particular, educational structures,[1] one of the slogans of which is 'grow together'. In China, the division of labour between the different social classes, between those who plan and command and those who carry out orders, is on the way to being abolished. All through his life, the intellectual

1. Johan GALTUNG, *Educational growth and educational disparity* [59, p. 18-19; 119n, p. 327], and especially the issue of *Prospects* containing articles on 'Aspects of education in China' prepared by Chinese authors [119o, p. 480-503].

will work regularly, for certain periods of time, as a farmer in the country or as a worker in a factory. 'Teachers and students go together for participation in productive work in a factory, a farm or a people's commune' [119o, p. 482]. Workers and farmers come to teach in the schools, education being closely linked to productive work (see p. 151). The schools are all wide open to society. 'The strageties of the Chinese approach are: to raise the floor of schooling by giving everybody pre-primary education (nurseries, kindergartens) and the middle-school system (lasting a total of ten years); and to lower the ceiling by cutting down on university education (to three years, out of which only eighteen months are theoretical training)' [119n, p. 327-8]. Individual examinations have been abolished.

If we included the Chinese curve in our Diagram 6, it would become almost horizontal; that is at least the goal of Chinese policy. Unfortunately, we lack the necessary detailed information to measure the results of these efforts, although we have a feeling that they would greatly upset all traditional conceptions and reveal gigantic forces and movements at work.

The qualitative aspect

The purely quantitative aspect of the problem of access to education is only one side of a much more complex situation. Beneath the rates of school attendance expressed in easily comparable percentages are hidden real facts which are often not comparable at all. Obviously, these facts are very difficult to come by. However, we have tried to give a few indications of characteristic disparities in Tables 2 and 3.

How to broaden access to education

During the last few years, a number of measures aimed at facilitating access to education, particularly higher education, have been worked out and put into practice in certain countries.

The first measure which is necessary is—as we have already seen in part—the construction of schools, the increase of seating capacity at all levels, the training of qualified teachers; in short, the expansion of the entire education system. For many developing countries, this is the first problem they have to solve. In spite of all efforts, universal school attendance is an objective which will certainly not be achieved by the end of this century.

TABLE 2. Expectations of school life (in years).

Country	Year	Expectation of school life in relation to total population		Expectation of school life in relation to educated population	
		Boys	Girls	Boys	Girls
Argentina	1962	8.2	8.1	8.9	8.8
	1965	8.7	8.7	9.2	8.9
	1968	8.9	9.1	9.4	9.3
Belgium	1959	9.9	9.2	9.9	9.2
	1962	10.6	9.7	10.6	9.7
	1965	11.0	10.1	11.0	10.1
	1968	11.3	10.5	11.3	10.5
Benin	1965	3.0	1.3	6.6	6.6
	1968	3.0	1.3	6.8	6.5
Botswana	1962	3.5	4.4	9.4	7.1
	1965	4.6	5.6	9.1	7.9
	1968	5.4	5.8	8.9	8.5
	1971	5.3	5.6	9.4	8.7
Bulgaria	1965	10.0	10.2	10.0	10.2
	1968	10.3	10.3	10.3	10.3
	1971	10.6	10.8	10.9	11.0
Burundi	1969	2.7	1.1	6.6	5.5
Central African Empire	1965	5.4	1.7	7.2	5.7
	1968	5.9	2.3	7.6	5.9
Chad	1966	3.1	0.7	7.7	5.4
	1969	2.5	0.7	8.1	5.5
Costa Rica	1964	8.3	7.8	8.3	8.0
Cuba	1965	7.9	7.9	8.5	8.8
Cyprus	1965	7.1	6.3	8.0	7.4
	1968	7.6	7.0	8.9	7.7
	1971	7.7	7.4	9.4	9.2
Ecuador	1963	6.3	5.4	8.1	7.4
	1966	7.0	6.0	8.4	7.3
	1969	7.6	6.7	9.3	8.3
France	1961	9.5	9.6	9.6	9.7
	1964	9.9	9.9	9.9	9.9
	1967	10.1	10.3	10.1	10.3
Gambia	1960	1.5	0.6	7.5	5.8
	1965	2.5	1.0	6.5	5.6
	1968	3.2	1.2	7.3	6.4
	1971	3.3	1.3	6.5	6.8
Federal Republic of Germany	1964	12.2	11.2	12.2	11.2
	1967	12.2	11.2	12.2	11.2
	1970	12.8	11.4	12.8	11.4

Table 2. *(continued)*

Country	Year	Expectation of school life in relation to total population		Expectation of school life in relation to educated population	
		Boys	Girls	Boys	Girls
Greece	1962	9.1	7.6	9.3	7.7
	1965	9.9	8.2	9.9	8.2
	1968	10.3	8.7	10.3	8.7
Guatemala	1965	4.6	3.6	7.9	7.3
	1968	5.2	4.0	8.3	7.6
Hungary	1972	9.9	9.3	10.3	9.6
India	1961	5.4	2.4	7.0	5.4
	1964	6.0	2.9	7.0	5.5
	1967	6.4	3.2	7.4	5.6
Japan	1970	11.3	10.6	11.3	10.6
Jordan	1962	6.6	3.6	9.2	6.9
	1965	7.5	4.6	9.3	7.1
Republic of Korea	1965	8.4	7.0	8.4	7.0
	1968	8.8	7.1	8.8	7.3
Kuwait	1962	7.5	6.0	8.6	8.0
	1965	9.0	7.5	9.0	8.9
	1968	8.2	7.9	8.2	9.4
	1971	8.8	8.2	9.6	10.3
Malaysia, Sarawak	1961	6.3	4.1	8.4	7.2
	1964	6.9	4.7	7.8	7.1
	1967	7.8	6.0	7.8	6.9
	1970	6.7	5.2	7.2	6.4
Malaysia, Western	1968	7.3	6.1	7.6	6.5
Mauritius	1962	8.1	5.9	9.1	6.7
	1965	7.7	6.0	7.8	6.4
	1969	7.8	6.4	7.9	6.7
Mozambique	1966	3.5	1.8	6.2	5.1
Netherlands	1961	10.0	8.9	10.2	8.9
	1964	10.2	9.2	10.5	9.2
	1967	10.7	9.6	10.9	9.6
	1970	11.2	10.0	11.4	10.0
New Zealand	1965	10.3	9.7	10.3	9.7
	1968	10.5	10.0	10.5	10.0
	1971	10.6	10.0	10.6	10.0

(continued)

TABLE 2. *(continued)*

Country	Year	Expectation of school life in relation to total population		Expectation of school life in relation to educated population	
		Boys	Girls	Boys	Girls
Panama	1965	8.9	8.7	9.5	9.5
	1968	9.0	9.0	10.0	9.9
	1971	10.1	10.0	10.2	10.0
Peru	1965	9.3	7.2	11.1	9.7
Portugal	1963	7.4	6.4	7.5	6.4
	1966	7.4	6.4	7.4	6.4
	1970	8.5	7.8	8.5	7.8
Spain	1966	8.3	7.2	8.9	7.8
	1969	9.3	8.2	9.3	8.2
Swaziland	1967	6.4	5.7	9.9	8.4
	1970	7.3	6.5	9.9	8.9
Sweden	1963	10.7	10.3	10.7	10.3
	1966	11.6	11.0	11.6	11.0
	1969	12.3	11.8	12.3	11.8
Togo	1967	5.5	2.1	8.5	7.4
	1970	6.5	2.6	6.8	5.6
United Kingdom	1961	9.5	8.9	9.5	8.9
	1964	9.8	9.2	9.8	9.2
	1967	10.1	9.5	10.1	9.5
	1970	10.3	9.8	10.3	9.8
United Republic of Cameroon	1971	7.5	5.1	8.8	7.5
United States of America	1960	13.1	11.6	13.1	11.6
	1963	13.4	11.9	13.5	11.9
	1966	13.8	12.4	14.0	12.4
	1969	14.3	12.7	14.4	12.7
Upper Volta	1964	1.2	0.5	7.5	5.2
	1967	1.4	0.6	8.6	6.4
Socialist Republic of Viet-Nam	1969	7.2	5.7	7.4	6.6
Yugoslavia	1960	9.5	8.2	9.5	8.2
	1965	10.5	9.1	10.6	9.5
	1970	10.2	9.2	10.2	9.5

Source: Unesco. *The dimensions of school enrolment: a study of enrolment ratios in the world.* Paris, 1975. (Current studies and research in statistics.)

TABLE 3. Systems of education: duration of compulsory school attendance; duration of primary education; age for beginning this education

		Number of countries in each major area						
		Africa	North America	Latin America	Asia	Europe and USSR	Oceania	Arab States
Length of compulsory school attendance	*Number of years*							
	5	—	—	1	5	—	—	—
	6	9	—	12	9	2	—	3
	7	2	—	1	2	—	—	—
	8	6	—	5	4	16	1	3
	9	3	—	6	2	9	2	2
	10	3	1	1	—	4	2	—
	11	—	—	—	1	4	—	—
	12	1	1	—	—	—	—	—
No compulsory school attendance		17	—	—	13	—	1	5
Unspecified		2	—	—	5	1	—	5
Total number of countries		43	2	26	41	36	6	18
Length of 1st level education	*Number of years*							
	4	1	—	—	4	2	—	1
	5	2	—	2	12	5	—	2
	6	19	1	17	23	10	2	14
	7	12	—	2	1	2	2	—
	8	6	1	3	1	10	2	1
	9	2	—	1	—	4	—	—
	10	1	—	1	—	2	—	—
Unspecified		—	—	—	—	1	—	—
Total number of countries		43	2	26	41	36	6	18
Entrance age for 1st level education	*Entrance age*							
	4	—	—	—	—	1	—	—
	5	5	1	6	6	5	3	2
	6	30	1	9	25	18	3	12
	7	7	—	11	8	11	—	4
	8	—	—	—	1	—	—	—
Age not specified		1	—	—	1	1	—	—
Total number of countries		43	2	26	41	36	6	18

Source: International Conference on Education, thirty-fifth session, Geneva, 1975. *A summary statistical review of education in the world 1960-1972.* Paris, Unesco, 1975. [ED/BIE/CONFINTED.35/Ref.2].

The consequences of what is commonly called the 'oil crisis' and the sudden slowing down of economic growth have resulted in a stagnation or reduction of the national budgets in both the developing and the industrialized countries, which is appreciably hampering the expansion of education.   Moreover, education itself is often very unequal within these countries.   Such disparities are particularly pronounced wherever the schools are more dependent on local authorities than on a centralized administration. The poorer communities do not have the same resources as the rich ones.[1]

There are other material problems which should not be neglected, especially in the poorer countries. To democratize access to education, it is not enough to build schools and train teachers.   In addition, education, including school materials (books, etc.), must be free. In underpopulated areas, it is necessary to organize the pupil's transportation (school buses) and give them a noon lunch (see p. 159). Systems of scholarships are also necessary.

Algeria, in its report to the thirty-fifth session of the International Conference on Education (1975), wrote the following:

Educational authorities have not overlooked the fact that the real democratization of Algerian schools is not limited to opening the doors wide to all the children in the country. The social origins of each child strongly influence the conditions under which schooling takes place. It has come to light, in fact, that a badly fed or undernourished child cannot have the same chances of learning as a child coming from a well-to-do family. As a step towards limiting these inequalities, a large programme has been introduced consisting of: grants and loans for school equipment; instalment payments for school textbooks; and an increase in the number of school canteens.

In France, it is expected that textbooks will be provided free of charge throughout the whole period of compulsory education by the school year 1980/81.

At that same session of the International Conference on Education, a widespread discussion took place on the question of access. While some delegations stressed the fact that access to education, and especially to higher education, was primarily a financial problem to be solved by creating classrooms, by introducing a system of scholarships, etc., others thought that, in spite of their complexity, those material aspects were less decisive in the long run than the question

1. OECD, *The educational situation in OECD countries* [102, p. 22-4].

of the motivations which induced young people to continue their studies. In some developing countries, it has often been found that the children of illiterate parents, or of parents who have received only a limited education, either do not attend school or are not sufficiently motivated to succeed in their studies.[1] In poor areas where there is compulsory education, an even more serious problem is often found: truancy. In this connexion, an OECD report notes the following:

... the burden of compulsion is more severe for poor parents than for those better off, and in some countries where average income is low (as it is in Southern Europe), there is still a substantial amount of truancy and illegal employment of children, just as there was in Northern Europe some decades ago when incomes were lower [102, p. 22].

Closely linked to the question of motivation is that of orientation and guidance. This is playing an increasingly important part in efforts to democratize access to education. In some cases, guidance is even beginning to replace the selective examinations (or 'guidance by failure'), which are one of the principal reasons for inequalities. 'If democratization is considered as a process of maximizing the abilities and education of all students, it is clear that the process is inhibited by examinations, especially by external examinations', as we can read in a book published by Unesco [80, p. 162]. And Torsten Husén notes that inequalities continue to exist—if they do not become worse —in a strongly selective and competitive system [68].[2]

The problem of the conditions for promotion obviously varies according to the levels in question. Although there is an obvious trend towards abolishing examinations for promotion from primary school to the first stage of the secondary school—naturally, the problem does not arise in systems in which the 'common core' extends to the end of compulsory education—the examination for promotion from the first to the second stage of the secondary school is still very widely used. However, there is a tendency to make this

1. See in this connexion: International Conference on Education, thirty-fifth session, Geneva, 1975. *Final report*. Paris, Unesco: IBE, 1975. [73d, p. 12].

2. Concerning the subject of tests, we might add the pungent remark of Professor J.R. ZACHARIAS (United States of America): 'I have often referred to tests as the *Gestapo* of education systems. Uniformity and rigidity require enforcement, so I have chosen a most denigrating title for the enforcement agency. Its hallmark is arbitrariness, secrecy, intolerance and cruelty' [119l, p. 43].

selection no longer on the basis of an examination, but rather on the basis of a continuous assessment of acquired knowledge and progress.

In Dahomey,[1] pupils are simply promoted to the next stage within the same school.... On the other hand, there is no process of selection between the two stages in Canada and the United States, where promotion is automatic. In South America, almost all countries have adopted the system of straightforward promotion following a review of the year's marks.... In the most modern educational systems of North America, there is a trend towards methods of 'continuous progression'. The teaching is also individualized in the sense that each pupil goes gradually through the entire stage without having to study at the same pace as his fellow pupils. With this method, the ideas of 'marks', 'promotion', 'failure' and 'repetition' are done away with [80, p. 64-5].

In Quebec, the current educational reform, which resembles those in other provinces of Canada, is particularly interesting and significant in this connexion.[2] This reform as a whole has been deliberately planned with a view to democratization: 'Quebec has chosen to revise its educational policies on the basis of the democratization of education.'

Quebec has opted for a system of comprehensive schools. At the elementary level, the 'grade class' has been replaced by the 'subject group'. There is no longer any question, therefore, of organizing a class in the traditional sense of the word, once and for all, at the beginning of the year. Various working sub-groups are set up within groups of the same age as often as the pupils' progress requires, on the basis of criteria which take account of the need for the integral and continuous training of each child. The primary criterion, the child's age, is weighted by others, such as his rate of learning, maturity, group affinity.

The same system is found again at the secondary level. There too the pupils are grouped together by subject. These groups are composed of pupils who have reached the same level of development with regard to the subject in question. The groups may be set up for a specific period of time, which does not necessarily correspond to the length of the school year.

A pupil is not forced to repeat all the courses in a grade if he has failed once or twice. After a failure, the pupil is not always obliged

1. Today the *People's Republic of Benin.*
2. We summarize here some information contained in 'The policy and planning of education—Canada' [13, vol. 3, p. 110-15].

to repeat the same course; he can choose another course which is consistent with his scholastic profile. The school commissions can organize compensatory and refresher courses for pupils who experience difficulties in their studies.

Thanks to the establishment of comprehensive schools, pupils are no longer forced, upon leaving elementary school, to go to different sections or to schools restricted to a special programme. They all meet again in the secondary school, where they are given a general course together, subject to a variety of choices.

According to an evaluation made by the Ministry of Education of the Government of Quebec, this new structure has brought about the following major changes: the removal of horizontal and vertical partitions between study programmes; flexibility in the guidance structures, which, by permitting a variety of options, prevents the students for as long as possible from having to make an irreversible choice; greater attention to the over-all education of the students by a wider extension of educational objectives.

Comprehensive schools are not found in Canada only, but also, as far as compulsory education is concerned, in Japan, Sweden and Norway; they have also been established to a certain extent in France and Italy. Denmark and Finland are now organizing a reform of their education systems along these lines [102, p. 25]. Of course, the establishment of such systems raises important problems with regard to organization, financial resources, the number and training of teachers and the teaching itself.

Today, it is generally recognized that the selection of young people, or the recommendation that they follow some specific line of study, should be delayed as long as possible in order to equalize opportunity of access to higher levels of education and prevent these young people from embarking on careers which, in the long run, would not be in keeping with their aptitudes or ambitions. For example, wherever the school structures have not acquired a degree of internal flexibility comparable with that of the comprehensive schools, bridges must be built between the different branches for those who have taken the wrong turning, as well as coaching, retraining or 'second chance' systems. 'Whenever somebody drops out of the education boat, he must be an extremely good swimmer ever to get back on board again', as Louis Emmerij very rightly says [119i, p. 333]. It is accordingly necessary to build enough life rafts. Diagram 7 illustrates a system in the pure dualist tradition. On the one hand, the *gymnasium* which leads to higher education; on the other, technical and voca-

tional education. Recent reforms, such as, for example. that of the
Federal Republic of Germany (see Diagram 8),[1] are characterized by a
search for increased flexibility and greater permeability between the
different branches. Wherever necessary, supplementary or coaching
courses or classes are organized.

DIAGRAM 7.   The education system in Greece as it was in 1970.

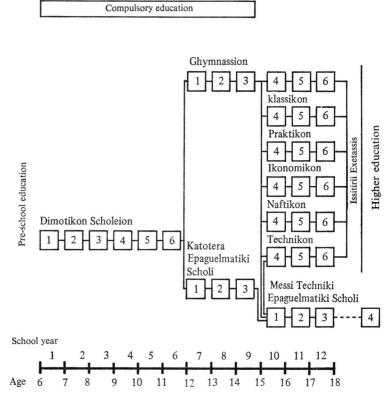

Source: Council of Europe. Council for Cultural Co-operation. *School systems:
a guide.* Strasbourg, 1970, p. 119. (Education in Europe. Section II: General and
technical education).

DIAGRAM 8. The education system in the Federal Republic of Germany.

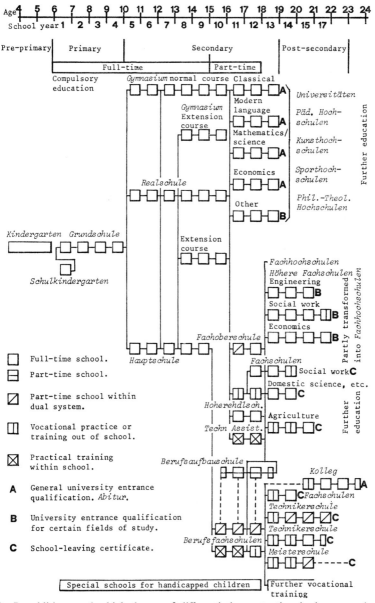

1. In addition to the high degree of differentiation, attention is drawn to the bridges between *Hauptschule*, *Realschule* and *Gymnasium*.

One of the most widespread and most important institutions of the 'second chance' kind is the evening course (for example, the evening *gymnasia* found in many countries, or the higher technical schools that are fairly common in Switzerland).

To a certain extent, all out-of-school educational activities can be considered as a means of making up for an educational deficit. All are additional roads to learning and offer new educational opportunities. Wherever education systems are underdeveloped, these opportunities are often of cardinal importance. Eminent specialists even defend the theory that in developing countries out-of-school education is more important because it is better adapted to the needs of those societies than the school of the traditional type, which was imported by the former colonizers.

Admission to university
and higher education

The degree of democratization of an education system is very often judged by the percentage of university enrolments in relation to the population of the corresponding age group, as well as by the breakdown of students by social origin.

As was shown in Diagrams 4 and 5, the number of students has increased very considerably in all areas. In eighteen out of twenty-four of the member states of OECD, the number of university enrolments has more than doubled during the decade and even tripled in three of them: France, Greece and Sweden [23, p. 16]. There has been an even faster increase in enrolments in non-university higher education. We are justified, therefore, in beginning to speak about mass higher education.

When we analyse the social origin of these students (see Table 4), the result is less spectacular. However, in spite of the fact that, from this point of view, the trend is clearly slower, it must be admitted that the democratization of access to education is beginning to show results.

Nevertheless, these developments are also causing certain imbalances: an imbalance with respect to the disciplines chosen (see Diagram 9), an imbalance with respect to career prospects, an imbalance with respect to the available openings for students. There is a danger that this latter circumstance may seriously affect the conditions for access to higher education, especially in certain European countries. Some countries have already found themselves obliged to introduce the

Table 4. Social origin of students in eight European countries.

	Year	Socio-professional categories [1]					
		A	B	C	D	E	Others
England and Wales	1961	61.0	13.0	—	—	26.0	—
	1970	46.0	27.0	—	—	27.0	—
Finland	1965	32.1	29.3	17.3		19.9	1.4
	1970	27.3	20.3	23.0		21.3	8.1
France	1960	55.2	34.4	5.8	—	4.6	—
	1968	47.0	30.7	6.3	—	11.9	—
Federal Republic of Germany	1961	34.2	29.0	3.6	14.7	5.4	—
	1970	26.2	35.7	4.2	14.3	12.6	—
Netherlands	1961	42.0	47.0		—	8.5	—
	1970	37.0	49.0		—	14.0	—
Norway	1964	33.6	11.1	12.0	—	23.9	—
	1969	37.6	11.0	7.5	—	19.5	—
Sweden	1950	55	39	—	—	6	—
	1960	48	39	—	—	13	—
	1968	40	37.4	—	—	22.6	—
Yugoslavia	1960	40.1		26.5	—	17.5	3.0
	1969	21.5	28.8	20.2	—	20.5	9.4

1. Classification (except for Sweden)—A: Higher category; B: Middle category; C: Independent farmers; D: Other independent workers; E: Lower category.

Source: OECD. *Towards mass higher education* [23, p. 30].

numerus clausus for a few disciplines, particularly medicine. It goes without saying that decisions of this kind have repercussions on an education system as a whole and may counterbalance efforts towards democratization.

In spite of this situation, which is critical in some places and generally aggravated by a shortage of resources, there are some countries—even European countries—which are continuing to reform their systems of higher education with a view to facilitating access to them. Higher education is being greatly diversified [38] and made more flexible in order to meet the increasingly different needs of their societies more effectively. In this connexion, special attention should be drawn to the trend towards creating short study cycles.

DIAGRAM 9. The development of enrolments in universities of Arab countries.

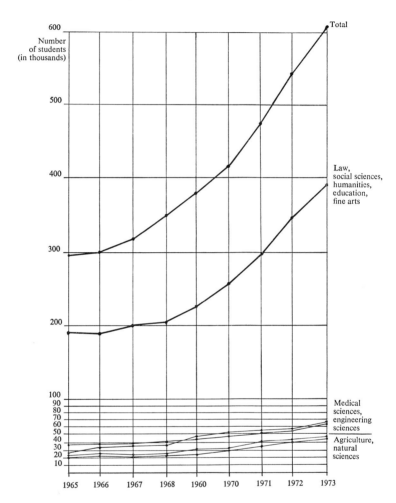

One innovation aimed at liberalizing access to university education deserves mention here. This is the example of Sweden, whose Parliament adopted a text in 1975 which regulates admission to universities in a new way.[1]

1. See: Britta ERICSSON, *Admission to tertiary education in Sweden* [52], whose text we have quoted in part.

In Sweden today, the general condition required for admission to higher education of the university type is completion of three or four years of the second stage of secondary studies. In some cases, candidates who fulfil certain special conditions are also accepted. In addition, by way of experiment, persons more than 25 years of age with at least five years of professional experience can enrol in a limited number of courses. This general rule is supplemented by provisions specifying the special knowledge required for various disciplines. In all cases, the candidates must have some knowledge of English.

Approximately 2,000 students of more than 25 years of age were admitted to university under these conditions in the departments of literature, social sciences and natural sciences in September 1975; this represents about 16 per cent of the total enrolment.

The new rules on general conditions are mainly based on the principle that ability is more important than diplomas. The result is that the general conditions for admission to higher education can be fulfilled in various ways.

If the number of candidates is higher than the number of available places, a selection has to be made. In principle, the selection can be based either on the estimated aptitude for study or on aptitude for a profession. Experience has shown that it is difficult, if not impossible, to measure satisfactorily by means of tests whether an individual possesses any aptitude for the future exercise of a profession. It is the aptitude for study, therefore, that constitutes the essential criterion when selecting candidates for post-secondary education. This aptitude will be measured on the basis of the marks received while attending school. Persons who have no school records can ask to take an aptitude test.

It has been considered important that candidates should be able to add additional points to the marks they received while attending school. School marks alone should not be decisive in determining the opportunities for access to higher education. It is also important that a considerable number of candidates should already have some experience of working life.

In many cases, early experience in active life can furnish a more solid basis for choosing a field of studies. The fact that previous work experience is taken into account can also be considered an important factor in developing a system of recurrent education.

All kinds of experience in active life, including bringing up a child at home, count for so many points, provided that the experience has lasted for at least fifteen months. Points are given for any kind of experience in active life lasting for a maximum of five years. The rules are formulated in such a way, however, as to guarantee that a limited number of pupils will pass directly from secondary education into post-secondary education.

Candidates having special needs with regard to third-level education, either because they suffer from some handicap or for any other reason, can be admitted on a priority basis. These are the new rules in Sweden concerning access to complete cycles of higher studies.

One of the traditional means of facilitating access to education, especially higher education, is the granting of scholarships or loans. These arrangements, which are extremely important for democratization and which are becoming more common almost everywhere, are too well known to require detailed description here. Some countries have introduced wages for students. Concerning this subject, Henri Janne takes the view that

> . . . the pupil or student, however old, is in fact pursuing an activity which will contribute to the social product by raising the intellectual level and qualifications—in the broadest sense of the word—of future participants in economic life. The pupil or student should be treated as the equal of a worker as soon as his formal education has stopped [131, p. xiii].

It should not be forgotten that the granting of a scholarship or a loan often does not solve the financial problems faced by a poor family when one of its children is pursuing his studies instead of earning money.

The concept of democratization and equality in education continues to gain ground. A few years ago, it was almost exclusively limited to the problem of access to education. Today we are going further. The concept of equality of access to education is being broadened to include the equality of opportunity to succeed in studies.

PARTICIPATION

Towards the end of the sixties, the great debate about participation opened with the force of a bombshell—in the notorious May '68 ! Today, we may wonder whether those events opened the way towards new horizons or whether, in the last analysis, they did not lead to a certain retreat to more traditional thinking. This violent, perhaps over-emotional and excessively irrational movement—did it not lose its original impetus by resorting to too much brutality and by arousing too many confused and ambiguous ambitions ? Obviously, it has had many concrete results. The flare-up of student action and the insistence on democratization have given students increased influence in the universities almost everywhere in Western Europe and even elsewhere [104, p. 67-8, 78, etc.]. But once the students were admitted to the various decision-making bodies of the higher educational establishments, their enthusiasm calmed down. On the whole, their participation was counterbalanced by a failure—often due to the lack of participants or of any really active participation. To give only one example among so many others, Botidar Pasavić noted the following in a report on participation in planning in Yugoslavia:

The official participation of students on school boards did not always mean their actual participation in planning and decision-making; lack of knowledge, teacher-student relations based on certification and authority, traditional family education of the students, etc., often made them only passive witnesses of educational planning and decision-making in schools. In many instances when they intervened it was not on strategic questions but rather to solve individual cases and minor interests [104, p. 128].

Participation is one of the principal features of any democratization of education. There can be no educative democracy without participation. However, it is strange to find that at the present time, this participation is much more the subject of philosophical reflections, ideological discussions or declarations of intent than of practical concern. As a participant in a European symposium recently said: 'Most countries were engaged in research on participation in education'.[1] Another author noted the following in this connexion: '"Participation" has become a catchword in many countries'.[2] And even in Sweden, according to the testimony of one representative of that country, 'the co-influence bodies in which pupils participate have very limited decision-making power.... Swedish school democracy as sketched in the curriculum must therefore be looked upon partly as an ideal goal, a target that has yet to be reached'.[3]

1. André de PERETTI, Symposium on 'Participation in Education and Training for Participation', Brussels, 1973. *Report* [138, p. 3-6].
2. Konrad von MOLTKE, *The consequences of participation* [111, p. 89].
3. Magnhild WETTERSTRÖM, *Research findings in school democracy in Sweden* [104, p. 181].

The problem would seem to be a very simple one. It would seem to be limited to the following question: how can we give the pupils on the one hand, and the community on the other, i.e. those who undergo, who pay for and who profit by education, a certain influence over their school? This kind of participation has always existed.

Ever since there have been schools, it has existed almost everywhere, especially in villages, which are administered by the local authorities. This is the case in England and Wales with their 'local education authorities', most of whose members have to stand for election every four years.[1] In Canada, the local authorities decide all questions concerning educational facilities, staffing, management of institutions, educational programmes, supervision and the systems for delivering educational services;[2] in Switzerland, the local communities appoint the teachers and decide what financial resources should be made available to their schools, which, incidentally, are administered by elected boards. In some developing countries, there are similar systems or experiments in progress in which the responsibility for educational institutions is entrusted to the local communities. Moreover, the ministers of education of the African Member States, meeting in Lagos at the beginning of 1976, stated, in a Recommendation adopted by the Conference, that they should 'organize schools that they may eventually become self-managed and self-financed units'.

An experiment in the self-administration of a university is under way in Denmark at the University Centre of Roskilde. This centre, which admitted its first students at the beginning of the 1972 term, has 1,200 today. Situated thirty kilometres from Copenhagen, it is separated from an area containing other educational establishments, including the University of Copenhagen. It maintains good relations with the local community, which is often associated in its work.

Like the Universities of Oxford and Cambridge, that of Roskilde is made up of students' houses, although the students do not reside in them. The centre also has a general library, two specialized libraries, a bookstore, meeting halls, a cafeteria and administrative offices. Each house accommodates about sixty students, six teachers and a secretary; in addition to the classrooms, it has a dining-hall and a

1. Roy P. HARDING, *Participatory aspects of local education planning in England and Wales* [104, p. 157].

2. Lyle H. BERGSTROM, *Some observations on Canadian experience in educational planning* [104, p. 101].

small lecture hall. Decisions concerning the organization of work and the granting of credits are taken at weekly meetings held in each house. The central administration is also based on a democratic system in which students, teachers and the non-teaching personnel participate on an equal footing.

Contrary to the customs in other universities, the *abitur* (school leaving certificate) is not required for admission to Roskilde. In fact, 20 per cent of the first-year students and 14 per cent of the second year benefit by this exemption, especially in the field of the social sciences, where this percentage amounts to one third. Their influence in the university is generally appreciated and they can, if necessary, take coaching courses.

Each teacher is responsible for directing the work of a certain number of student groups, but he may be consulted by other groups. Experience has already proved that teachers at Roskilde must avoid excessively narrow specialization and be familiar with the methods of group dynamics.

The work is organized in the form of projects carried out by groups composed of the students of a given house. The topics are freely chosen on the basis of the programme. Instruction consists of a first basic cycle, lasting two years, followed by a second cycle which varies in length according to the speciality. The basic course offers three electives (natural sciences, humanities, social sciences), but aims particularly at interdisciplinarity. Work in groups obviously makes it possible for all participants in a project to evaluate both the methods used and the results, while other evaluations are made at various levels.

If in villages—for in cities the situation is different because it is often almost completely inpersonal—the local authorities, and especially the parents, have always taken an active part in the life of their schools (like the teacher, who normally plays an important part in the social and cultural life of the village community), the pupil himself has never been a purely passive and non-participating element either. He is always taking part in school life. And even if he has no official decision-making power, he exerts some influence on the school system, on teaching activities and on the decisions taken by the teachers or by the authorities. There is always interaction between teacher and pupil, for their roles are always reciprocal.

At first glance, the problem of participation in education may seem commonplace. It would seem to be simply a matter of dividing up the decision-making power between the parties involved.

In actual fact, however, the question is extremely complex, and it is not surprising that all the implications of this concept are not really known. What is its real meaning? Does it change according to political ideologies? Does it mean participation within the school system or outside it, in other words, does it mean the participation of the students (May '68 and what followed) or of the parents? Who should participate in what and how? Who—pupils, teachers, administrators, parents, 'society', politicians, political parties, trade unions, ideological groups, professional circles—or all of them together? And in what—managing the school, defining the objectives of education, planning education systems and activities, drawing up programmes (general or individual), outlining teaching methods, teaching, evaluation? Just to think of the possible interactions—beneficial or disastrous for the school—between all these questions (the list of which is far from complete) will give some idea of the complexity of the matter.

In addition to this, any problem of participation is not only a political question, but also and primarily a question of power and the division of power. It also involves the question of the status of the teacher and his relations with the pupil. It is therefore also a question of choosing an educational approach. In this context, however, one must bear in mind that mere legislation is not enough to translate changes of this kind into facts.

Nevertheless, we can single out a few key ideas. One of the first is this: there can be no participation without decentralization.

A second idea is that a democratic school, managed by the community, is everybody's school. It is therefore not only the school of the young people (or of the teachers), it is the centre of all the educational activities of a community. It is a school which is open to society and it is a school which is really integrated with society. This is the school that the delegate of Algeria was talking about at the thirty-fifth session of the International Conference on Education, when he said that 'if the school is really integrated in the village, the young people are not going to leave the village to go and work in the city'.

THE DEVELOPMENT
OF SCHOOL INFRASTRUCTURES

A careful analysis of the new school architecture would reveal all the present trends in education. Social structures and their projection

FIGURE I. 'Kolumbus' school in Berlin-Reinickendorf: a school without corridors. Each class has a space for open-air teaching. 1. Classroom; 2. Space for open-air teaching; 3. Gymnasium.

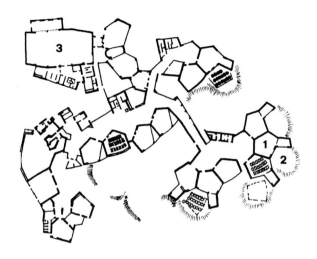

FIGURE II. Secondary school at Mariemont, Ohio (United States of America) composed of hexagonal units. Teaching areas are not separated from each other. 1. Teaching area; 2. Teachers; 3. Closed-off room; 4. Administration; 5. Library.

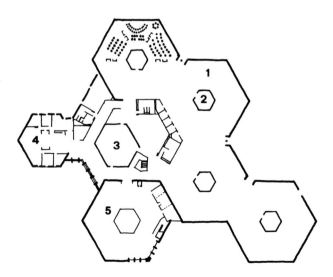

FIGURE III. Prototype school developed by Unesco and the Regional Institute for School Construction in Africa. This model is based on a complex of three classes grouped around a central common area. This layout allows rational use of the outlying areas for group activities: plays, film projections, etc. 1. Classroom; 2. Open-air teaching space.

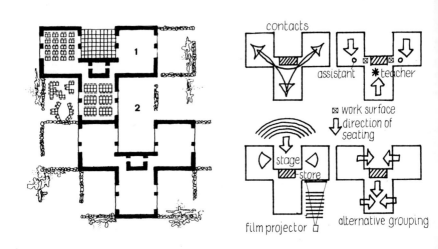

FIGURE IV. A Unesco project for an experimental school at Sukarnopura (Indonesia). This school virtually cost the price of an axe and a few packets of nails. It is designed on a circular plan without a central feature, which allows the teacher to check on the different groups of pupils spread around the school. The plan allows several different positions for the tables and blackboards; they can also be placed on the outside.

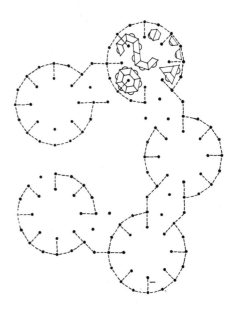

FIGURE V. School at Vesterøy (Norway). A flexible model for a small school (100 pupils). 1. Teachers; 2. Lockers and showers; 3. Central hall; 4. Teaching space.

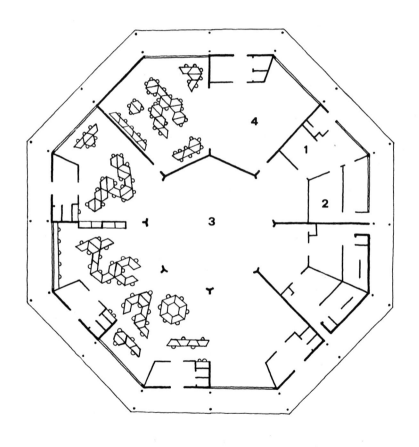

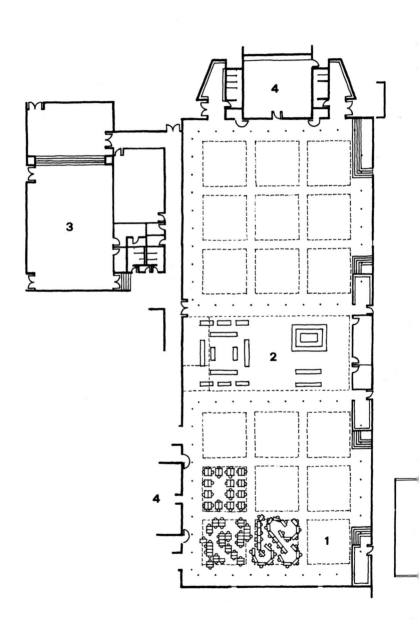

FIGURE VII. Primary school at Memphis, Tennessee (United States of America). The architects explain that the design of the school is based on four principles: (a) organization of study around the individual, learning being acquired individually; (b) mixing of various levels and subjects, stimulating collective contact and research; (c) the absence of a time-limit on study for all age groups; (d) dynamic teaching necessary for community development. 1. Teaching area; 2. Classroom with movable partitions; 3. Library; 4. Enclosed space.

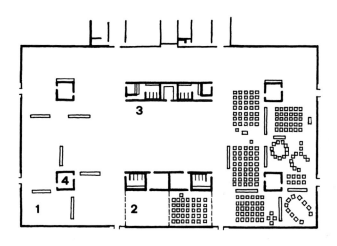

FIGURE VIII. Education centre at Rodenkirchen (Federal Republic of Germany). All teaching areas are set out in different ways. 1. Area for group teaching; 2. Individual work; 3. Teachers and equipment; 4. Teaching area for very large groups.

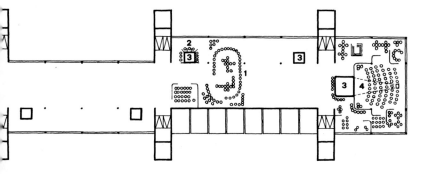

FIGURE IX. A mobile learning centre in an old bus.

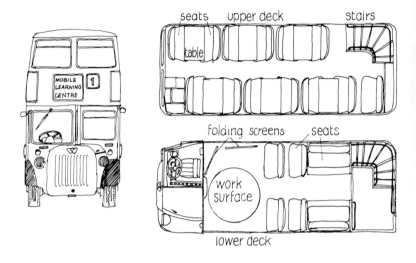

FIGURE X. Project for an educational and cultural centre at Brunswick (Federal Republic of Germany). The scheme is designed around an 'education street'. In such an educational development, does the pupil become the educational consumer? 1. Swimming pool; 2. Living accommodation; 3. Old peoples' homes; 4. Social services; 5. Library; 6. Secondary school; 7. Indoor sports; 8. Outdoor sports; 9. Primary school; 10. Old peoples' recreation centre; 11. Forum; 12. Leisure centre.

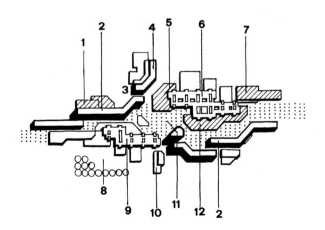

FIGURE XI. Mobile dividing unit and sketches showing its flexibility for different teaching situations.

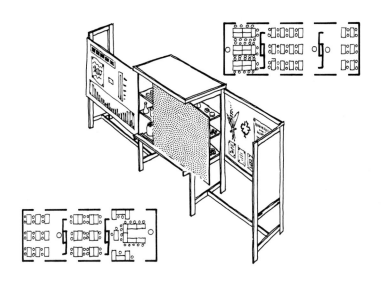

FIGURE XII. An open-air literacy class at Vidyapith school, Mysore (India).

FIGURE XIII. The library of St Louis Priory school, Missouri (United States of America).

FIGURE XIV. L'école des plants constructed in 1971 at Cergy-Pontoise (France). (Photo: J. Renaudie.)

in the future, community ambitions and educational approaches are directly reflected in the main skeleton frame, organization of space and external appearance of school buildings. The plan of a school is both an educational project and a project of society. It is a dialectic similar to that which characterizes the relations between education and society: architecture is an expression of the society which, for its part, it contributes to form. School building plans reveal as much about the educational and political intentions of the school authorities as do the outlines of education systems. Architecture is a projection of these outlines in space. Consequently, a careful study of architects' blueprints is just as instructive as reading a long account of the development of education and teaching.

Wherever education is on the move, school buildings are changing their appearance: where are the old school barracks with their gloomy courtyards behind high walls which cut the school off from any contact with its environment? Where are the large buildings, slightly pompous, austere, rigid and pretentious which were attended by the future élites of the nation? Even the traditional country school, as found in Switzerland, for example, is disappearing—a neat, trim building as befits such a serious and respectable enterprise as education, but with red flowers on the window-sills and the teacher's family garden behind the yard, with its cabbages and lettuce. The good old school which, together with the church, marked the centre of the village is hardly built any more in that style which makes one think of the starched shirts of the farmers.

School buildings have joined the march of progress; they have burst out in colours and have opened up like giant flowers to take on increasingly imaginative shapes. From the old rectangular plan, with long corridors and classrooms lined up like soldiers, they have moved on to increasingly free groups of annexes and other architectural elements, sometimes recalling bee-hives or sets of multi-coloured cubes. This all goes to show the liberation of teaching and the change in the relations between teachers and pupils. We have begun to build schools for children who are supposed to learn by playing; in other words, by remaining children and not being forced to behave like adults.

As we have already noted, there continues to be greater flexibility in education systems, greater emphasis on making them more open and mobile, inside and out. When rigid classes were abolished, the traditional classrooms also began to disappear; their walls became movable or were eliminated altogether. They are being replaced by various arrangements of teaching areas. Now the school has opened up to the surrounding world, and now education systems, which had formerly been fixed and petrified in specific age classes and sections, have been broken up into study groups which come together, separate and come together again freely, according to the educational needs of the pupils. Architecture, therefore, will have to find physical solutions to give practical form to these new learning styles.

About ten years ago, the first schools were built of the kind in which the whole school body occupies a single space, like certain modern administrative buildings where everybody, from the director down to the typists, works in one open-plan office. The pupils study there in groups. Library, collections of objects and television set are within easy reach. Each pupil is free to make his own way through this educational open space, both literally and figuratively. The class teacher has been replaced by teaching teams.

From what we have described in the preceding chapters, it is clear that schools of this kind are to be found particularly in Canada, as well as in the United States, the United Kingdom and the Scandinavian countries. After the first experiments of this kind, it was realized that the large, single space—there are cases where as many as fourteen 'classes' work in a single, completely open room—should, nevertheless, possess a certain structure.

In Canada, a preliminary evaluation has been made of this new type of school [14]. On the whole, the results are favourable. Most of the children there seem happier and more relaxed. Comparative studies of the scholastic results are not yet completed, but the general impression is that schools with large areas give at least as good results as schools of the conventional type. However, there are some pupils— and also some teachers—who prefer the more intimate atmosphere and sense of security to be found in a closed room, where one feels 'at home'. The experiments completed up to now show that, with this system, the best solution seems to be a large, open but structured area, surrounded by a few closed rooms, or rooms which can be easily partitioned off, which are reserved for the teachers, for film showings, music exercises, language learning, scientific experiments or certain kinds of manual work. There is also a theatre and a gymnasium.

The logical end-result of this trend is probably the 'school without walls' which we find in the United Kingdom and the United States in particular. In an old bus, for example, a 'mobile learning centre'. Formal education has been completely replaced by a learning process which can be carried on anywhere at all: outdoors, in a factory, on a work-site, in the theatre, museum or zoo, in front of a radio or television set, in the street, at home—and even in a classroom.

As we have just seen, the new teaching and educational structures, which are more open, more free, more active, which are based on the group work and team work of pupils and teachers, and at the same time more individualized and linked up with the search for a democratization of education, are reflected in the only architectural forms which can make their implementation possible. The other major trend in education today, closely linked to the first and complementary to it, is the attempt to give practical effect to the concept of lifelong education. This concept is also influencing new studies in school-building construction.

From the point of view of lifelong education, the traditional school, which was reserved for children and for a particular category among them (primary and secondary school pupils, etc.) is being transformed into an educational and cultural centre open to the entire community. In addition to school establishments of various kinds and levels, these multi-purpose educational complexes contain facilities for adult education, leisure centres, youth clubs, libraries, social centres, etc. Sometimes they form small towns of their own, built along a main 'education street'. They are real cities of education.

Chapter Four

Education and society

There is nothing new about asking what role education plays in society.
All philosophers who have pondered over questions of education have
done so, from Plato (in *The republic*) to Jean-Jacques Rousseau, from
Wilhelm von Humboldt—who thought that the formation of a well-
organized personality (*die wohlgebildete Persönlichkeit*) could not and
should not take place except when removed from social constraints—
to John Dewey, who, in his book *Democracy and education*, considered
that we were far from realizing all the constructive possibilities inherent in education as an agency for the improvement of society.[1]
Today, a very lively debate is going on, especially in the liberal countries, about the dependence of education systems on social systems, as
well as about education's contribution to society and its transformation. For several years, it has been one of the favourite subjects of
sociologists and very much in fashion with all those interested in
educational theories. This problem does not seem to arise for the
socialist countries, since they take it for granted that education is a
direct emanation of the socio-economic system.

The fact that relations between education and society, and especially between the school and society, have for some time been
becoming a problem may mean that education is no longer as well
integrated with society as in former times. But it may also mean, as
some claim, that the societies in question are in a state of crisis.

Here, we cannot undertake an analysis in depth of the complex
relations and interactions between education and society, or attempt
to sum up all the theories and ideologies which have dealt with this

1. See: Robert ASHCROFT, *The school as a base for community development*
   [111, p. 28].

topic during the last few decades. We shall confine ourselves to sketching a few outstanding features of current thinking on this subject, and then go on to describe in somewhat greater detail four important aspects: relations with development; relations with the world of labour; the special case of populations in rural areas; and, lastly, the cultural aspect.

One of the most controversial questions is who is changing whom; in other words, whether education can change society or whether education systems are entirely dependent on social systems—in which case it is first necessary to change society in order to change education later on.

According to the first argument, education is the fulcrum of Archimedes from which it is possible to move an entire society. According to this school of thought, a society's future can best be influenced through the school, for it is the school which shapes those who will be responsible for tomorrow. That was the leading idea of the *Aufklärung*, which incidentally is repeated in the famous sentence in the Constitution of Unesco: 'Since wars begin in the minds of men, it is in the minds of men that the defences of peace must be constructed...'. It is by education that society is changed, that society is able to carry out new projects; it is by education that we have a hold on the future. Education, therefore, must be organized in conformity with the kind of future we hope to have. For example, it is through the democratization of education that we will create an egalitarian and truly democratic society; it is by abolishing classes in the schools and by giving everybody equal opportunities to receive as uniform an education as possible that we will finally abolish social classes. This conception of the transforming role of education is summarized by Gabriel Fragnière as follows:

> ... the critical impact of knowledge, with its ability not only to transform the physical environment but also to call in question the structure of society and how it functions, is by its nature revolutionary and a source of social change. (The determination of repressive authorities to clamp down on all education which leads to criticism is itself a proof of education's power in this respect.) At the present time it is this hypothesis of the educational system as an agent of transformation which is being verified.[1]

---

1. Gabriel FRAGNIÈRE, *Creative education* [56, p. 28]. In his preface to this book Henri JANNE writes: 'When society finds itself on the threshold of great changes, education ceases to be a mere reproduction of the past: it becomes *creative*.'

Extract from the introduction to the *Unesco medium-term plan* (*1977-1982*), p. xxx.

Education ... should play a decisive part in preserving or giving fresh significance to men's relationships with their environment and with the communities to which they belong. All too often, education appears to do just the opposite, thus leading to alienation. This is sometimes the case, in the developed and developing countries alike, when education seems to be cut off from the important things of life and consequently tends to create passivity and indifference. Ways of remedying such situations depend, of course, on having policies adapted to the cultural conditions and objectives of each society. However, among the efforts to make education more meaningful and to integrate it more closely with the real life of society, attention should be drawn to measures designed to associate productive work with education. Such programmes may make an important contribution to the renewal of educational curricula and methods, forge closer links between intellectual and manual occupations and enable young people, through productive work, to contribute to the development of their society and even to create resources which help to cover the cost of their education. This is but one example of the sort of education which would foster creative capacities.

Education which stimulates social awareness and public participation to tackling communal problems helps to increase the ability of each people to produce new ideas and create new resources and techniques; it also facilitates the latter's utilization in the interests of society as a whole.

Amadou-Mahtar M'Bow

Although not all of them want to be revolutionary, most important educational reforms are originally based on a political will aimed at renovating society.[1]

The other argument conforms to Marxist theory, according to which an education system is a function and tool of the society which conceived it. A society, and especially its ruling class, perpetuates itself by and through education, by transmitting to future generations its systems of values, its codes of behaviour and attitudes, its knowledge and its 'truths'. It is by education that young people are gathered to the fold, formed in a particular mould and integrated with the social system. In the class struggle, the school becomes an instrument of repression of the ruling class, which practises a kind of 'colonialism' against young people. From this point of view, educational reforms in non-socialist countries do not aim at such ideals as justice or a real democratization; on the contrary, they are dictated solely by economic needs. If the capitalist society has opened the doors of its universities wider, it is because it needs an increasing number of highly skilled personnel and not because it is concerned about greater equity. The proof of this is the general failure of the efforts to equalize opportunity in education, efforts which fail to lead to any equal opportunities for success or to equality in jobs or careers.[2] From this point of view, an education system is an instrument of social control. Paulo Freire expresses this position very forcibly:

> There is a more or less widespread and naïve belief in the power of institutionalized education in transforming reality.... It is not systematic education which somehow moulds society, but on the contrary, society which, according to its particular structure, shapes education in relation to the needs and interests of those who control the power in this society.[3]

There is still another, more pragmatic position, which is disparaged by some as traditionalist and conservative, if not even reactionary. This position does not place the emphasis so much on society—which

1. See, for example: *Contours of a future education system in the Netherlands* [94].
2. Christophe JENCKS, notes in his book *Inequality*, which has made quite a stir: 'There is nothing in the data we have reviewed to indicate that educational reform can lead to social changes of any importance outside the schools' [77].
3. Paulo FREIRE, 'Literacy and the impossible dream' [119p, p. 68].

has recently been described in this context by a well-known author [1] as an allegorical personage in a play performed in a theatre where the ticket-offices are closed and the actors are the teachers, pupils, educational technicians and educational philosophers—but rather on the pupil, the individual. Education should be a social service, useful to the individual. A young person needs guidance in the world, but above all he needs knowledge and practical intelligence in order to find a job and earn his living. In this way he will be able to become a useful member of his community and contribute to the development of the society to which he belongs. From this point of view, the question arises whether the efficiency of the school is increased by allowing the political and ideological dissensions of our time to enter it.

As is well known, for some time now the school has been the subject of increasing criticism and disputes. The idea of deschooling society has become common currency. Above all, it is said that the school is no longer adapted to the needs of society, that it has not been able to keep up with the changes caused by the explosive progress of science and technology, the increasing social imbalances and the instability of the economic systems of the Western world. The needs of society are very seldom specified. Moreover, who could specify them and according to what criteria? The socialist countries claim to have solved these problems, since educational structures and programmes have been completely integrated with general planning. In China, the symbiosis between school and society seems to be complete. 'The whole of society has become one big school', says one Chinese author.[1]

However, in many developing countries, the question of the concordance between their education systems and the needs, structures and levels of development of the populations takes on a very special form owing to the fact that their education systems were not a natural creation of these societies themselves. They are foreign bodies, imposed on them during the colonial era—supplanting and covering up indigenous systems of learning—which they inherited at the moment of liberation. Their purpose was primarily to train the personnel needed to make the territories run smoothly; in other words, they are not at all suited to the needs of the present time, which are determined by autonomous political options and the requirements of develop-

1. Maurice REUCHLIN, in the Introduction to his book *Individual orientation in education* [125, p. vii].
2. YONG-HONG, 'The educational revolution' [119o, p. 481].

ment. The search for endogenous education systems, adapted to the present cultural and socio-economic realities of these countries, is one of the most urgent problems confronting us today in the field of education.

EDUCATION AND DEVELOPMENT

Slowly, much too slowly, mankind is beginning to realize the dangers now opposing it. Besides the threat of an atomic war capable of destroying the planet, other dangers have appeared on the horizon, such as the limits of growth and their consequences, the spectre of world famine and serious ecological risks. The famous reports of the 'Club of Rome' and the controversy about them have the inestimable merit of causing one to think. Among world problems as a whole, the growing inequalities between an affluent minority and a poverty-stricken majority, the serious imbalances between industrialized countries and developing countries, are a sign of flagrant injustice, a source of anxious concern and a constant threat to world peace. The problem of development is undoubtedly the most important, the most serious and the most urgent one now confronting humanity.

Inequalities

It is true that since the launching of the first Development Decade (1960-70), considerable progress has been made in a number of developing countries. 'Their rate of progress has been unprecedented, far exceeding the rates attained by the industrial countries at any earlier comparable stage of development' [99, p. 10]. However, the disparities between industrialized countries and developing countries have not been reduced; on the contrary, they have increased. The gap has continued to widen, for growth normally generates inequalities (see Diagram 10). These disparities have also become evident, and also continue to increase between the different developing countries, as well as within them, thus creating additional tensions. It is not surprising that progress is slowest in the most underprivileged areas, that the most wretched are the ones who profit least by progress.

In spite of certain undeniably favourable results, the situation as a whole is characterized by increasing uneasiness and anxiety. This is due, on the one hand, to the fact that the disparities have reached a point which is less and less tolerable and which may pose an increasingly serious threat to international peace; on the other hand, the

DIAGRAM 10.   Growth accentuates inequalities as long as it is not greater at the lower level than at the higher level.   Our graph shows curves of constant growth of 10 per cent, starting from different levels.

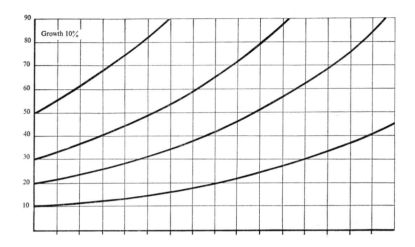

general situation has deteriorated since 1973: inflation and recession in the industrialized countries; the explosive rise in the price of oil (with its repercussions on many products, such as fertilizers); the instability of the monetary system and the deterioration of trading terms are being cruelly felt in the developing countries. As the problems confronting these countries are subjected to closer analysis, they seem to become increasingly more complex and more difficult to solve.

It is in this context that we should view the *Declaration on the establishment of a new international economic order* and the corresponding *Programme of action* which were adopted at the sixth Special Session of the United Nations General Assembly (1974), as well as the various negotiations in progress between developing countries and industrialized countries.

The various specialized agencies of the United Nations, as well as other international organizations, have been concerned with these problems of development for almost a quarter of a century. Most of them are also concerned about the establishment of a new international economic order. For its part, Unesco took up this question in 1974, when the General Conference, which is its supreme organ, adopted a long resolution on that subject at its eighteenth session. In a publication devoted to those questions, Amadou-Mahtar M'Bow, the Director-General of Unesco, stated:

As a Specialized Agency of the United Nations, Unesco was in duty bound to make its contribution to the world community in order to further thinking and activities designed to promote the establishment of a new international economic order and, at the same time, to play the part properly falling to it as an adviser on matters within its special purview. There can, in fact, be no question of a new and more equitable world order unless due heed is paid to the requirements of education, science and culture, and full advantage taken of the light they can throw on problems [150, p. 10-11].

The characteristic features of underdevelopment are generally known. It is human misery in all its multiple aspects: hunger, disease, ignorance, unemployment, poverty, precarious housing, etc. Everywhere in the world, this underdevelopment is found side by side with underdevelopment in education: low school-attendance rates at all levels, high rates of repeating and drop out, a very low average level of teacher training, high rates of illiteracy. It would seem, therefore, that there is a relationship between a country's level of general development and the level of development of its education system.

In search of relevant education

The developing countries have made a serious effort to develop their systems of education. 'The field in which developing countries have made their greatest efforts is undoubtedly education', states a report of the OECD [99, p. 60]. Some of them are devoting one-fourth or sometimes even one-third of their national budget to education. Consequently, there has been a very considerable increase in school enrolments (see p. 96). Since the beginning of the 1970s, however, this expansion has slowed down appreciably.

There was a time when development was practically identified with the growth of the gross national product. Since then, it has been realized that this approach was far too simplistic. Development does not concern the economy only; there are other factors of a social and cultural nature which are just as important. A country where injustice in all its forms holds sway and where the inequalities exceed certain limits cannot be considered as developed. It is the individual who is the final purpose of development; the individual in the enjoyment of all his fundamental rights as they have been codified in the Universal

Declaration of Human Rights. It is the welfare of the individual in the full sense of the word; it is the quality of life. However, this concept of development has undoubtedly not been sufficiently clarified, and the mechanisms which bring about and support development have been clarified still less. For this reason and, moreover, because the real influences exerted by education on society are very inadequately known, there is no way of evaluating the interactions between education and development with any precision. There can be no doubt that education alone cannot serve to trigger the process of development, but it seems equally obvious that education is an essential factor in any development of a society.

There are many countries which do not hide their disappointment with the results of their efforts in the field of education. They have invested enormous sums in it and the costs of education are constantly increasing; nevertheless, the national production has not advanced in proportion, social inequalities and imbalances have increased, the problem of unemployment, and especially unemployment among university graduates, is creating increasingly disturbing tensions; the flight from the land is becoming more serious; etc.

Analysing this state of affairs, responsible government authorities and research workers arrive at conclusions which are often identical, although they may sometimes differ. Their one common denominator is that they almost never question education as such, but rather the way in which it is conceived and organized. Briefly, as it is today, education seems to be poorly adapted to the needs of the developing countries.

Today, practically all developing countries and a good number of research workers are indicting the schools which were inherited from the colonial powers. In the report of the Conference of Ministers of Education of African Member States, which was held in Lagos at the beginning of 1976, we can read the following passage, for example:

> It is an acknowledged fact that the educational systems left over from the colonial period do not correspond to the political options of the new African States, to their geographical, physical and human situations, to the requirements of development, or to their resources. This raises the problem of the need to make education more relevant to the African national context. Education for whom, and for what purpose? [21k, p. 21].

It is true that these school systems were originally conceived by societies having a completely different level of development, that they transmitted systems of foreign values, that they imparted knowledge which was meaningless in such a totally different environment (I shall always remember the little boy I met in the middle of the African bush who told me how he had to study the music of the troubadours in school), that they were highly selective, that they prepared people primarily for auxiliary jobs in the colonial administration, that they cut the pupils off from their surroundings. Incidentally, there was a time when indigenous parents received payment for permitting one of their children to go to school.

Some authors wonder whether it is really justified to accuse the colonial school of all these evils. After all, those who criticize such systems so vigorously are all products of them themselves, and very successful ones at that. One research worker of African origin notes with some bitterness: 'In public African politicians talk of "Africanization". In private and in practice they express their preference for external services.' [1]

In this connexion, there is one phenomenon which we should not try to cover up: the voluntary importation of foreign models. Some countries have a tendency to choose—one is tempted to say 'à la carte' or according to the fashion—innovations which have proved successful but which were thought up in totally different socio-cultural contexts, or technologies developed for special situations, and to transplant them to their own shores as they are. In some cases foreign experts or consultants are responsible for such actions, but it also happens that the authorities in the countries in question insist on transferring foreign models, although warned against them by specialists on the subject. Naturally, it is always much easier to copy than to invent; and in questions of development, since the dazzling 'successes' of the industrialized countries and the example of the former colonial powers have left traces which are not so easily effaced, they continue to have a profound influence on the objectives and implementation of development policies in many countries of the Third World. The invention and creation of endogenous educational systems seems, therefore, to be closely connected with the search for really relevant models of development, adapted to the needs and aspirations of those countries.

The question of profitability

In the developing countries, economists question education systems about their profitability, about their actual contribution—if possible

1. Uga ONWUKA, *Western type education and the development of Africa* [18, p. 67].

in terms of figures—to development.[1] The replies are fairly ambiguous. Disturbed by the phenomenon of unemployment, and especially the unemployment and underemployment of young people who have had secondary or even higher education, they wonder whether the expansion of education systems in these countries might not lead to imbalances and create serious difficulties.[2] They wonder whether the money spent to train the unemployed could not be used differently and, as a first alternative, to create jobs. Educational policy should be much more intimately co-ordinated with policies in other sectors. Nearly everybody thinks that the developing countries are investing much too heavily in the higher education sector and not enough in the primary sector. If secondary education and higher education are too greatly developed, this is due to the fact that governments yield to social pressures, which always demand more education. After all, from the individual's point of view, education seems to be a good investment in any case. It is undeniable that the better educated a person is, the more likely it is that, if he can find a job, his job will be better paid than that of somebody with a lower level of education. Some economists, however, wonder why this should be so, as it is by no means certain that the degree of one's education has any direct effect on one's productivity.[3]

Unesco views these questions in a different light. It not only considers it of primordial importance for the developing countries that the broad masses of the population should have a minimum level of education and that those countries should be able to call on skilled workers, but it also stresses the fact that they will not succeed in solving their problems until they create their own scientific potential:

The speeding up of the growth of the scientific and technical potential of the developing countries is, from all points of view, an urgent necessity. While the importance of increasing the fundamental research potential, linked with the development of higher education, must not be neglected, attention must also be directed to the practical objectives of medium- and long-term development... [150, p. 66].

1. Concerning this subject, see: *Education and development reconsidered* [159], a work containing a whole series of contributions on this topic.
2. Concerning this subject, see, for example: Edgar O. EDWARDS and Michael P. TODARO, *Education and employment in developing countries* [159, p. 3-22].
3. Mark BLAUG has the following to say on this subject: 'We still know very little about the learning process in schools and even less about why schooling is so highly rated in the labor market' [159, p. 31].

The search for new models

The developing countries are looking for new models because they have noted the lack of relevance of their imported education systems and realize that the high cost of these systems will not permit them to educate all their population within a reasonable period of time. While doing so, they are beginning to recall their own methods of education which existed before the appearance of colonialism. Perhaps these countries had not had any schools, but all of them had had a highly developed practice in education.

The first result of this search for alternatives, which can also be found in the industrialized countries, is a tendency to separate the existing education systems from the schools.[1] For, first of all, it is necessary to break up the rigid framework of the school of the traditional European type if new forms of education are to be found. It is typical that these experiments in innovation are being made on a small scale. These are far from being pilot experiments in all cases, i.e. experiments deliberately designed to test some innovatory theory; very often they are projects which are born almost spontaneously. It is also typical of these new forms of education that they are directed almost more to adults than to children, for it is the adults, particularly the young adults, who are the active agents of development, and they are the ones to be approached first of all if progress is to be accelerated. In almost all cases, these new forms of educational projects are aimed directly at the process of development, and very often at development in practical, local conditions. Because of their different characteristics, it is hardly possible to transfer these experiments to another environment.

A typical example of the flexibility and adaptation of school structures in a village context was to be found in Laos.[2] The financial resources of Laos did not permit it to include all its children in the conventional academic school system. For this reason, beginning in 1962, rural centres of community education (CREC) were created

---

1. In this context, see Ralph M. MILLER, *The meaning of development and its educational implications* [159, p. 83-93].

2. See: Kamphao PHONELEEO, 'The Laotian challenge: a non-polluting education system' [119l, p. 90], from which we have borrowed this passage almost word for word. In addition to the examples given by us in this section, a few others based on similar criteria will be found farther on, especially in the two following sections. Laos is now, of course, the Lao People's Democratic Republic.

in the villages; these CREC are at the same time lower primary schools (three years), youth centres and centres of basic adult education. A CREC may be either a pagoda school with the local monk for a teacher, or, in places where there is no pagoda, a rural school built by the initiative of the villagers themselves, with a local, part-time teacher who is chosen and maintained by them. The curriculum of the CREC is based on village life; essentially, what has to be done is to make the children understand the world about them, to see clearly the simple improvements that are needed in their village and to persuade them to initiate those improvements themselves. Through the problems of the village, therefore, taken as a focus of interest, both children and adults will learn to read, write and count, and, starting with their own village, they will gain some notions of history, geography, natural sciences, practical techniques and economics.

Several educational radio campaigns have been launched in the United Republic of Tanzania, a country particularly rich in novel experiments and which is deliberately favouring adult education because its influence on development is more immediate than that of the education of children.[1] These campaigns are based on the organization of radio study groups and supported by the simultaneous publication of booklets. Each campaign is devoted to a particular subject of immediate interest—health, increasing farm productivity, literacy, etc.—and accompanied by a special slogan and symbol. They last up to ten weeks. Study groups are formed spontaneously, especially in the villages. They are composed of persons of all ages and all conditions: men, women, young people, adults, the literate and the illiterate, farmers and artisans, meeting together on an equal footing. Usually, they themselves choose a chairman and/or a group adviser or animateur, who often follows a preparatory course before the campaign begins. What these groups mainly do is to engage in discussions, exchange ideas and experiences, with the encouragement of the radio broadcasts, and read publications together on the study topic. These studies very often lead to concrete projects, which are carried out either individually or jointly.

Quite another approach is that taken by Colombia, with its National Learning Service (SENA), and more particularly its system of mobile instructor units which go from village to village and give courses

---

1. See: Lennhart H. GRENHOLM, *Radio study group campaigns in the United Republic of Tanzania* [61].

in practical education.[1] These instructors carry all the necessary teaching material in their car (including audiovisual aids), but they also draw heavily on local resources. The courses, which on the average last for sixty hours, spread over several weeks, are on widely different subjects: agriculture, livestock, such as cows, rabbits and hens, as well as beekeeping, gardening, sewing, handicrafts, first aid, hygiene, etc. The methods are those used in practical learning, without too much theory. These courses are primarily intended for adolescents of both sexes.

The education of women for development

In most developing countries, fewer girls go to school than boys. However, women's contribution to development is especially important, above all in rural areas, and should not be underestimated. It is concentrated primarily in three essential fields: nutrition, health and education.

First of all, the women not only take care of the household and prepare the food, but they also often do the gardening and, in some Asian and African countries, cultivate the fields. It is the women, therefore, who are primarily responsible for feeding the family. It is consequently essential that they should be taught how they can make the best use of their food resources. We might add that it is also usually the women who go to market to sell the family produce.

In the second place, it is the women who look after family health and hygiene. This begins with contraception, which is something of the greatest importance in developing countries, where many problems are becoming increasingly and tragically more serious because of the population explosion. The fertility of women has been found to be directly linked with their level of education. However, women are also the first to care for illnesses in their families, especially those affecting infants and children, and it is they who are responsible for hygiene.

Lastly, the mother's role is decisive in the education of children and particularly for their scholastic success. This has been confirmed by many studies.

In short, the education and training of girls and women are perhaps more profitable for social development than that of boys and young

---

1. See: Philip H. COOMBS and Manzoor AHMED, *Attacking rural poverty: how nonformal education can help* [27, p. 46-8], a book which contains and analyses many examples. See also, by the same authors: *New paths to learning* [28].

men. Female education, therefore, should be encouraged for other reasons than those of equity alone. Many countries are becoming aware of this. Among them we should note certain Arab States which are now making special efforts to broaden the access of girls to education.

Special programmes for the education of women are being carried out in certain countries. One example is to be found in Upper Volta.[1] There, a broad educational programme has been started as part of a functional literacy project undertaken under the auspices of Unesco. One of its leading features has been health education. Some villages have established maternity hospitals and organized special courses which teach the local midwives to look after newborn babies properly and instruct the village women in the rudiments of child rearing. The importance of hygiene has been emphasized and sanitary installations have been improved. The women have been taught to make water filters to prevent drinking water from being contaminated, to improve the family diet and to carry out their household tasks. They have been trained to make better use of the available resources, to practise economy and to think up new sources of income, as well as to adopt more efficient techniques for gardening and poultry rearing, sewing and traditional handicrafts. Women have been encouraged to clear and cultivate collective fields under the guidance of group leaders, and in this way have acquired practical experience in community work, while learning to make proper use of fertilizers and seeds, to plant crops in rows and to use the best methods for storing. The villages have been supplied with radio receivers and groups have been formed to listen to and discuss broadcasts in the local language aimed at supplementing the community education programmes.

Basic education

In autumn 1974, a seminar of senior education and planning officials, organized jointly by Unesco and Unicef, was held in Nairobi. The topic discussed was basic education in Eastern Africa [133]. In the final report of the Conference of African Ministers of Education held in Lagos (at the beginning of 1976), a whole chapter was devoted to 'basic education', considered as 'a powerful means of development', and reference was made several times to that concept in the Declaration and Recommendations adopted by that Conference [21k].

1. See: Unesco, *Women, education and equality* [153, p. 17-32], from which we have obtained this information.

What is it all about? The Nairobi Seminar drew up the following definition:

Basic education is the minimum provision of knowledge, attitudes, values and experiences which should be made for every individual and which should be common to all. It should be aimed at enabling each individual to develop his or her own potentialities, creativity and critical mind both for his or her own fulfilment and happiness and for serving as a useful citizen and producer for the development of the community to which he or she belongs. ... basic education should enable young people: (a) to participate effectively through their work in the *economic* development of their country; (b) to contribute as citizens to national unity on the political, cultural and social levels through service to their community; (c) to develop their own personality.

What this amounts to, therefore, is a kind of minimum package of education, or what Coombs has called 'minimum essential learning needs' [28, p. 13].

The content of basic education is by no means a rigid programme. It is flexible; it must be adapted to special educational situations and rooted in the socio-cultural environment to which it is directed. Emphasis is placed on practical guidance and on the development of attitudes. After all, one of the paramount objectives of an education aimed at development, and therefore at productivity, should undoubtedly be to learn to work.[1]

Basic education is not acquired exclusively in the school. In this respect we see that this concept is based on autochthonous forms of education. Traditional African education was closely linked to the family and the village community, and it was practised in concrete situations of daily life. Transmitted by rituals and symbols, by tales and legends, by a whole arsenal of extremely varied educational methods, it was above all an initiation into the adult world and the working world.

The acquisition of education is not confined to a particular stage of life (for example, ages 7 to 14) or to a particular place. It represents the turning-point between the school and out-of-school education.

---

1. Mark Blaug writes: 'Schooling makes people more productive not just by imparting cognitive knowledge but also by "socializing" them in various ways: punctuality, achievement motivation, the willingness to take orders and to accept responsibility are no less vocationally useful skills than the ability to turn a lathe or to read a technical instruction' [159, p. 28].

But this is not to deny the importance of the primary school altogether. Having acknowledge that the primary school system was solidy established on the ground and in public opinion, the participants in the Nairobi Seminar nevertheless charge that it has six outstanding defects in the African context: (*a*) it is an imported product; (*b*) it is too expensive; (*c*) its main function is to supply candidates for secondary education; (*d*) it does not prepare the pupils for real life but encourages them to desert the rural areas and to despise manual labour; (*e*) its internal efficiency is mediocre; (*f*) it caters for only about one child in three [159, p. 23].

We might note in passing that the debate is far from closed between those who would advocate the deschooling of education and those who defend it. This debate is just beginning and will undoubtedly get even livelier. We can expect the parents to swell the ranks of the defenders of the school. That represents a danger for the concept of basic education, which might be weakened by those who would regard it as a cut-price education.

As we have already noted, basic education, as understood at the present time, is characterized by very great flexibility in every respect. It is rightly to be regarded as the primary component of an over-all system of lifelong education. But it is this very flexibility which will make its implementation difficult. For it is an extremely complex task to plan an education system in which formal education and nonformal education are not only complementary but also in part parallel, while at the same time providing for certain bridges between them.

Development education

The development of the Third World does not concern only the poor countries. It is a matter of concern for mankind as a whole. Solutions to this whole set of problems can be found only through co-operation and solidarity. Unfortunately, broad strata of the population have not yet understood what is at stake, and certain political events are not having a favourable influence on public opinion. In the liberal democracies, however, co-operation with the developing countries will depend on this public opinion and on every single individual. For this reason, information and educational campaigns should be carried out at all levels to make young people and adults understand the necessity of combatting the tragic injustices and inequalities which are dividing countries and peoples. These campaigns should begin in the school. Development is one of the major contemporary problems which should be the subject of studies at all levels of education. Moreover, young people are receptive to these problems, and youth organizations such as Unesco clubs are very actively concerned with them. For example, we read the following in the manifesto of a youth organization in France: [1] 'We call on the governments of developed countries to educate for development, by ensuring that the teaching world is open to the problems of under-development, and by including economic and social training and reflection on under-development in official syllabi.'

Education about development takes various forms: education for understanding between peoples and international co-operation and solidarity; the teaching of the historical causes of underdevelopment; an awareness of the major world problems, interrelations and inter-dependences between industrialized countries and developing countries, as well as the injustices characterizing the world of today, etc. To an increasing extent, this teaching is breaking away from a tendency to be too 'exotic' and is taking a more critical approach to these problems, starting from the fact that underdevelopment is a phenomenon found in all countries of the world, whether industrialized or not, and which highlights a need for change in the present world order, as well as within national societies.

THE SCHOOL AND THE WORKING WORLD

The school and the working world are two fields which, to a large extent, develop independently of each other and which are governed by their own laws. After all, on the one hand, there is a considerable number of unemployed and underemployed workers who have not only received a basic education but also have school-leaving certificates and often even university diplomas, while on the other hand, in many countries there is a shortage of skilled personnel, particularly in the fields of technology, science and management. These facts constitute two elements in a strikingly paradoxical situation. And yet, these two worlds ought to be intimately connected. For no social, economic or cultural development can proceed harmoniously unless there is broad agreement between education and the working world. 'Integrated development' should mean nothing else.

1. French National Youth Commission for the World Hunger Campaign. Quoted in OECD, *Development co-operation* [99, p. 115].

In September 1975, a meeting was held at Unesco headquarters in Paris of Senior Officials from the Ministries of Education of the twenty-five least developed countries (LDCs). In their final report, they have the following to say on this subject:

Traditional educational systems, inherited from the colonial past and focusing on the training of white-collar workers, have created a situation whereby, in many of the LDCs, massive unemployment and underemployment of school leavers with an inadequate and irrelevant education coexist with a critical demand for a skilled labour force relevant to development needs. The employment crisis is thus the result of a mismatch between an educational strategy aiming mainly at quantitative expansion of the academic streams and an economic strategy which, until rather recently, focused on expansion of the modern sector which cannot absorb most of the academically trained people searching for jobs [86b, p. 5].

In the developing countries—and also in a large number of industrialized countries—the situation of young people who have completed their studies is a tragic one. There are many authors, representing all points of view, who violently blame the schools for this. But to claim that the school is responsible for unemployment is probably going too far. However, one might well wonder whether an unemployed educated person does not feel more frustrated than an illiterate.

Under these conditions, the question arises whether, at the present stage, the priority given to the extension of education systems by the developing countries is justified. Concerning the objectives of the Addis Ababa Conference, according to which 100 per cent school attendance should be achieved in the African countries by 1980, Joseph Ki-Zerbo writes the following: 'What is important to us is to know the direction of the rails before determining the power which we must give to the engine. Indeed, we must know if it is leading us to a garage, or toward a station, or toward a precipice. Happily, the present direction has reversed the approach which was envisaged at Addis Ababa' [119d, p. 418]. In this connexion, some authors think that 'most of the developing countries, although not all of them, are suffering from persistent under-investment in primary education, together with a no less persistent over-investment in higher education'.[1] Others go even farther and wonder whether they should not stop building

1. Concerning this subject, see: Mark BLAUG, 'Economics and educational planning in developing countries' [119d, p. 431-41], and 'Manpower forecasting as a *technique*, not an *approach* to planning' [119h, p. 458-63].

primary schools. In countries where expenditure on education represents between one-fourth and one-third of the national budget, there can at any rate be no question of increasing the existing school infrastructures to any appreciable degree. In any case, not in the next few decades.[1] They think that, in present conditions, universal school attendance would not only lead to dangerous frustrations, but would also waste considerable resources, i.e. that it would be much better to create jobs than to produce unemployed university graduates. 'Education is a priority sector, which ought to be stimulated, but which cannot be expanded indefinitely inasmuch as there is the risk of creating unemployment of educated individuals who would then, when meeting with frustation, create pools of dissatisfaction, apart from the implications in terms of investments lying idle or being under-utilized' [98, p. 50-1].

There is an obvious conflict between such arguments and the principle of the democratization of education and the Declaration of Human Rights—in any event as long as total school attendance is considered a condition *sine qua non* for the democratization of education. But authoritative voices do not hesitate to denounce 'the myth that only a school system which is the same for all children guarantees equal opportunity' [119g, p. 341].

The Director-General of Unesco, Mr. Amadou-Mahtar M'Bow, does not share this skepticism at all. He says so very clearly in a speech:

Now is the time to protest against a prejudice, which is unfortunately becoming more and more widespread, to the effect that education is to blame for the drift from the land and for unemployment. I think that this argument is both groundless and dangerous. It is groundless, because the highest levels of unemployment are to be found among the illiterate and those who have left school too early. It is dangerous, because it seems to justify a cut in the budget for education, thereby creating the risk of a reduction in educational facilities, which would have the effect of depriving all those whom modern knowledge leaves by the wayside of any opportunity to participate effectively in the transformation of their societies. To deprive the poor of education

---

1. Concerning this subject, see a study carried out under the auspices of Sheikh Hamidou KANE for a Unicef conference: 'Secondary education, training and employment: confronting the hopes of young Africans' [119g, p. 333-41], which contains the following sentence: 'But it will not be sufficient to change the schools and to refrain from establishing them in new areas...' [ibid, p. 335].

is to condemn them to eternal poverty. No society has ever suffered from too much knowledge or know-how. Education is still a driving force of social progress.[1]

Until the real interactions between education and economic development are better known, we must avoid trying to over-simplify the problems, especially since economic reasoning is certainly not the only kind of reasoning which applies to education. However, the present systems will undoubtedly have to branch off in new directions. Only too often the school is conceived of in the light of some visionary economic situation, i.e. some purely hypothetical situation, and it will have to be better adapted to the harsh necessities of the working world. But socio-economic systems will themselves have to be transformed so as to be better able to meet the legitimate aspirations, including the cultural aspirations, of mankind.

In the industrialized countries with a liberal economy, the unemployment of intellectuals is also a sign of what could be called 'over-education' due, among other things, to the democratization of education. The unemployment of intellectuals goes side by side with a lack of unskilled workers, and as a consequence we find that those countries are importing workers from less developed areas, who are often illiterate. That whole problem is very different from the one met with in the developing countries. In the long run, it will have revolutionary repercussions on the division of labour in the industrialized countries.[2]

With very few exceptions, the active populations in almost all countries of the world are divided into two categories: the intellectual workers and the manual workers—those who conceive, plan and give orders and those who carry out the orders—the 'white collars' and the 'blue collars'. The former acquire social prestige (but not always high salaries); only the latter are usually regarded as workers.

The school is regarded as a means, or even *the* means, to provide access to the higher steps in the social ladder. Even today, the level of studies completed, the level of examinations passed, the prestige of diplomas and academic degrees, seem to be the main factors on which

1. Speech delivered at the Tripartite World Conference on Employment, Income Distribution, Social Progress and International Division of Labour [144, p. 2].
2. Concerning this subject, see: Aldo VISALBERGHI, et al., *Education and division of labour* [157].

professional success, careers and social success depend. This is the principal reason why everyone wants to climb to the higher levels of the educational hierarchy.[1] To respond to these pressures, the higher levels are made accessible to all; education is democratized and the same opportunities are given to everybody—and the race to happiness or prestige begins all over again in the higher stage !

Louis Emmerij, a senior ILO official, has described pertinently and with humour:

...the cannibalistic tendencies that exist in the education system. By this I mean that the lower levels of education tend to prepare the pupils mainly for the next higher level of education rather than for the world of work outside the education system. It is in this sense that one can say that education eats its own products and those who are not swallowed by our mammoth have difficulties in being absorbed anywhere else. Put in other words, the education system in most countries concentrates in terms of its content and structure on the very small minority that continues to the higher levels of education and is much less concerned with the majority for whom primary or secondary education will be terminal [119i, p. 333].

At the beginning of 1976, the African ministers of education met in Lagos. Conscious of the problems to which we have just referred, they defined one of the priority tasks of the school as follows: 'To provide a new form of education so as to establish close ties between the school and work; such an education, based on work and with work in mind, should break down the barriers of prejudice which exist between manual and intellectual work, between theory and practice, and between town and countryside' [21k, p. 30].

The transition from school to active life is a crucial and particularly critical moment in the life of every individual, since this transition is from adolescence to adult age. In traditional societies, this transition was the key moment in education, characterized by rites of maturity and initiation.

Today, the turning-point between the school and the working world is one which deserves very special attention. Serious tensions

1. A Soviet newspaper, *Izvestia*, had the following to say on 1 March 1971: 'Eighty per cent of the young people who apply to the employment office of Krasnodar District have failed their entrance examinations for higher education. They are not interested in the working conditions. For them, the most important thing is to be able to prepare for the next competitive examination' [119g, p. 410].

can arise there—and some of them already exist. To a large extent, the development of both the Third World and the industrialized countries will depend on whether there are smooth relations between the school and the working world.

Education for work [1]

In the traditional European education system, the school is carefully separated from the working world. This is due in part to a nineteenth-century reaction against the exploitation of children by developing industries. The school protects the pupil from the working world for a certain number of years. Man's life is stratified into two periods: school and active life. After the period of compulsory schooling, a choice is made between the 'good' pupils, who are permitted to continue their studies, and the others, who are forced to work. The latter move into the production process, while the former are trained for a profession. In this system, the teachers never come into practical contact with the working world.

This model is still very widespread throughout the world. However, it is possible to discern a pronounced tendency to take advantage of technical and vocational education and to introduce an aspect of technological education in general education, especially in programmes during the first stage of secondary education. In many countries, especially in the non-European areas, they go even farther by introducing productive work in the school.

Certain trends are clearly apparent in Western Europe. For example, we find the tendency to create a common core going as far as the end of compulsory schooling and gradually introducing, besides those subjects which are compulsory for all, a more or less large number of options, in order to help the pupils to choose a profession. With regard to the second stage, this has been expanded by integrating technical and commercial subjects leading to diplomas upon the completion of studies which are comparable to the school leaving certificate (*baccalauréat*). On the other hand, there is a great reluctance to inte-

1. 'The relationship between education, training and employment with particular reference to secondary education, its aims, structure and content' was the special topic of the thirty-fourth session of the International Conference on Education held by Unesco: IBE (Geneva, 1973). The working documents of this conference and its final report are full of information on these questions. See also the book by Jean THOMAS: *World problems in education* [143, p. 37-56].

grate vocational education (in the strict sense of the term) with the second stage of secondary education.[1]

In these same countries of Western Europe, there is a very clear tendency 'to postpone the moment of specialization as long as possible and to offer instead a more polyvalent technical and vocational education that will make possible relatively rapid adjustment to a range of jobs or occupations that require one fundamental course of training. It seems preferable that specialization, or adaptation to a particular job or work post, should take place on the job, in a firm' [129, p. 19-20].

The question of the choice of an occupation raises the problem of job forecasting and, above all, that of pupil guidance. Although some authors, like Mark Blaug, take the view that 'manpower forecasts of the long-term variety are such as to render them almost indistinguishable from wild guesses' [119d, p. 433], there are some countries, on the contrary, which do not hesitate to apply very rigorous planning in this field. In these questions, the differences between opposite socio-economic systems become particularly obvious. According to a Soviet author,[2] in the USSR 'there is a considerable discrepancy between the intentions of senior pupils as regards their future employment and the manpower requirements of the economy'. The great majority of young people would like to enter university at all costs. 'In connexion with the training of manpower for the needs of the economy, the guiding of pupils towards manual employment is becoming a serious matter for the State. . . .'. For this reason, 'vocational guidance consists chiefly in imparting to the adolescent (taking into consideration his individual characteristics, of course) a particular vocational orientation, which will be determined by the manpower requirements of the economy'. Accordingly, the educational method of vocational guidance consists primarily of preparing 'young people for working life—for work in general and also for the choice of a particular occupation. . . . The educational approach requires that the young man should choose an occupation which interests him and for which he has an inclination, but it also requires that the interest and the inclination should not arise by the chance operation of random, uncontrolled factors but should take shape as the result of a purposeful educational influence brought to bear on him over a considerable

1. See: Paul SCHLEIMER, *A panorama of technical and vocational education in Europe 1962-75* [129, p. 14].
2. See Y.P. AVERIČEV, 'Guiding school pupils towards manual occupations in the USSR' [119g, p. 372-9], the source of all the quotations given in this passage.

period of time, taking into consideration the personal characteristics of the individual and the manpower requirements of the economy.' Preparation for choosing an occupation, therefore, consists of awakening 'a positive attitude towards socially useful work'. The pupil must be imbued with 'a communist attitude to work and a respect for the working class', and should be encouraged 'to choose industrial employment'.

In the countries of Western Europe, the concept of guidance is based on the pupil's personality and on freedom of choice. This concept is now developing in three main directions. First, the moment for choosing an occupation is postponed for as long as possible so that young people will not have to take this decision, which will be critical for their future, until they are sufficiently mature to realize the consequences of it. Secondly, guidance is becoming an aspect of education as such. 'The concept of the function of guidance has been enlarged to include a psychological aspect and an educational mission. Seen as an educational process designed to cultivate the ability to take decisions, it is an essential part of education, and thus an integral part of any educational system' [129, p. 25]. Thirdly, guidance is being aimed less and less at the choice of a specific occupation and more and more at a branch of education. Inasmuch as jobs are becoming increasingly diversified and the number of persons who change jobs during their lifetime is constantly on the increase, it is essential for the individual to develop the ability to adapt himself to changing job situations.

It should be added, however, that it would be an illusion to think that the choice of an occupation can depend exclusively on purely individual considerations. 'There is a widespread public acceptance of the idea that the primary purpose of education is to train the individual for a vocation' [125, p. 62], and people are not satisfied with vague goals aimed exclusively at the 'full development of the personality'. Any guidance, therefore, is strongly influenced by the situation on the labour market, although it must be admitted that this mechanism is always considerably behind in producing its effects. For its part, the *numerus clausus*, which is being applied in universities more and more, very seriously reduces the freedom of choice, which nevertheless remains an ideal of non-socialist societies.

Education through work

Long neglected, the educational value of work is being increasingly recognized—reluctantly in the industrialized countries with a liberal socio-economic system, but more emphatically in the socialist countries and in many developing countries. In a publication of the Council of Europe, Paul Schleimer writes: 'From an educative angle, increasing importance is being attached to practical work, especially manual work. Apart from their specifically vocational values, such exercises are now seen to offer a wide range of general educational possibilities, long unrecognized and still not fully exploited' [129, p. 19].

'In present conditions, the integration of productive work with teaching and education constitutes one of the general trends in the reorganization of education', we read in Bulgaria's report to the thirty-fifth session of the International Conference on Education.

The links between education and work should not be examined solely from the point of view of the organization of school studies and the adaptation of their subjects to future jobs; they should also be considered from the point of view of direct co-operation between education and the employment sector. This co-operation, which is mutually advantageous for both parties, may take various forms at various levels, from the participation of the industrial sector in deciding what subjects are to be taught to direct ties of practical collaboration. In the Eastern European countries, for example, where every secondary school has contacts with one or more enterprises, which often help to equip its workshops and laboratories, the enterprises often send specialists to participate in vocational guidance and also in certain classes, and all pupils spend several hours a week actually working in those enterprises, performing tasks corresponding to their studies.

In the *Final report* of the Conference of African Ministers of Education, Lagos 1976, we find the following passage: 'Work is an essential component of development, and the African of the future must be a worker, a producer. These concepts were downgraded in the imported school and the new school must reinstate them in a place of honour. The incorporation of manual work into education therefore has an educational significance, as it is by producing that a pupil learns to be a producer within a community itself committed to the effort of production' [21k, p. 22].

The dichotomy between a general, theoretical and literacy education—the 'white collar' education—and vocational training—of the future 'blue collar' workers—is therefore in the process of disappearing. In the long run, it will yield place to new forms of formal and non-formal education. The new educational centres which are being established in different parts of the world are both places of teaching and centres of production at the same time. There are many cases where experiments are being carried out in integrating education with work. Among these examples are the village polytechnics in Kenya (see p. 166), the revolutionary educational centres in Guinea,[1] the Swaneng Hill School in Botswana,[2] the mobile vocational training schools in Thailand, the development school learning centres found in Indonesia,[3] the young people's camps in Jamaica, the system of learning associated with formal education in Colombia, etc. These are often 'micro-innovations' of recent origin which have been introduced on an experimental basis to solve the problem of the connexions between education and work: comprehensive schools, in-service training, community schools and other attempts to adapt structures and programmes to the local environment. In such cases, the results of these innovations still have to be assessed, as well as the possibility of applying them generally and on a large scale.

However, apart from important plans for educational reforms aimed at establishing close ties between education and work, such as those in Peru or those in the African countries like Benin, Ethiopia and Togo, there are some projects which have actually been carried out on a large scale. They include those in Cuba, Yugoslavia and especially China, all of which seem particularly interesting. The Cuban example, with its secondary schools in the countryside, will be described in a later section (p. 163-4); here we will give a very brief account of the other two.

For almost twenty years, the community schools have been the basic element in the education system of Yugoslavia.[4] These schools are closely linked to the local communities, which to a very large extent assume responsibility for them. One of the fundamental principles of these schools is 'workmanship combined with polytechnical education and the linking of learning with productive labour and other work useful to the community' [8, p. 6]. They are based, therefore, on the educational value of work and participation in the process of production.

---

1. See: Galema GUILAVOGUI, 'The basis of the educational reform in the Republic of Guinea' [119o, p. 435-44].

2. See: Patrick van RENSBURG, 'Swaneng Hill School' [16, p. 158-72].

3. See: *Educational innovation in Indonesia* [70, p. 36-9].

4. See: Stevan BEZDANOV, *A community school in Yugoslavia* [8].

These community schools are open to adults who wish to supplement their general education. In this connexion, Stevan Bezdanov makes an observation which deserves quoting:

> The relationship and co-operation between the school and the local community do not entail a lowering of educational standards to the level of the local community, which, in underdeveloped areas, might tend to be backward, but rather an adjustment, where the school is the active factor and promoter in the fight against backwardness. The school stems from the commune and originally it bears all characteristics of its background; then it raises these characteristics to a higher level and, by its reciprocal influence, makes its impact on the community from which it stems. This applies to rural as well as to urban communities [8, p. 5].

In the community schools of Yugoslavia, the pupils are engaged—besides participating in the productive work of enterprises—in improving the environment. They plant trees, look after green areas, mow public lawns, etc. In the Sonya Marinkovic School in Zamun, in the suburbs of Belgrade, which is described in detail in the publication mentioned above, the children of the seventh and eighth grades work in the local factory for four hours once a week over a period of two months [8, p. 22].

In China, education is organized according to the principle formulated by Chairman Mao: 'Education should serve the policy of the proletariat and should be combined with productive work' [119o, p. 481]. Undoubtedly, nowhere else in the world has work become such an integral part of all educational activity and nowhere else does the significance of education follow so directly from the process of production. In China, work and education are blended together in a single political design. School education is no longer limited to the classroom.

In town and country alike, primary and secondary schools have established links with the factories, peoples' communes and army units in the neighbourhood. Where the required conditions obtained, small factories and farms have been set up in primary and secondary schools, and workers, peasants and soldiers have been invited to teach on a part-time basis. In the universities, a new threefold linkage has been introduced, closely associating teaching, scientific research and production.... Universities also have their own factories and farms.[1]

---

1. The review *Prospects* devoted its last issue in 1975 to education in China. Our information and quotations are taken from this 'dossier' [119o, p. 482].

Attached to the University of Pekin, for example, is an electronic instruments factory where ultra-modern calculators were developed.

After the secondary stage, every young Chinese spends at least two or three years in active life before he can continue his studies. University students are recruited among workers, farmers or soldiers possessing a school-leaving certificate and upon the proposal of the local Party organization. The State decides what branch the student will enter, on the basis of his aptitudes and, above, all of its job requirements.

Another educational model aimed at removing the wall between the school and the working world is that of recurrent education, which we have already discussed (see p. 56-60). It will be recalled that its main characteristic is the alternation between periods of study and periods of work. This system, therefore, also includes the search for greater flexibility in adapting general education and vocational training to economic situations and to shifting and increasingly unstable job conditions.

EDUCATION IN THE RURAL WORLD:
THE RURALIZATION OF EDUCATION

Scope of the problem

Education in rural areas poses one of the key problems of development and of the future of mankind. It is a problem of enormous dimensions. And like every crucial problem, it is extremely complex.

At the present time, approximately 62 per cent of the world population, or nearly 2,500 million human beings, are living from agriculture, this includes 1,500 million who are young people of less than 24 years of age. By the year 2000, the agricultural population will pass the 3,000 million mark.

Three persons out of four in the totality of developing countries live in rural areas. In the United States of America the opposite is true. There, only one person out of twenty-five is a farmer

In the least developed countries, 80 to 90 per cent of the active population work in agriculture. In those countries, agricultural products account for almost all exports [99, p. 71-5].[1] 'The question

1. Examples: Ethiopia (98 per cent), Sri Lanka (97), Gambia (96), Chad (94), Upper Volta (88), Thailand (82), Honduras (81)—1970 figures.

of bringing rural areas into the mainstream of modern civilization is at the heart of the battle for development, which is the major battle of humanity in our time', said René Maheu, the former Director-General of Unesco.[1] The few figures we have just cited show what a tremendous battle this is.

A few characteristic features of the farmers' situation

Throughout the Third World, the rural areas are the least developed. It is there that we find the heaviest demographic pressure, the highest rates of unemployment, under-employment and illiteracy. These are the areas which suffer most from malnutrition, lack of hygiene, poverty and misery. There, transport and communication facilities and power distribution networks are completely inadequate. There is a flagrant lack of institutional infrastructures.

Almost everywhere, the rural world is an isolated world, turned in on itself. Social relations and the organization of production are often archaic. Consequently, the average productivity of agricultural work is low.

The broad masses of the farmers are imprisoned in a vicious circle of poverty, hunger and ignorance. These undernourished peasants have neither the physical strength nor the intellectual ability and necessary knowledge to free themselves from their misfortune. The most underprivileged among them are the small farmers, whose productivity has a tendency to decline, in spite of certain successes of the 'green revolution'. Almost everywhere, the rural world is a world in stagnation. In Unesco's publication, *Education in the rural environment*, we find the following description of the rural society:

In a world closed in upon itself, subjected to the rhythm of the seasons and the crops, no difference is drawn between one form of work and another. In this world all forms of occupations are social obligations necessary for the preservation and cohesion of the group. Concentrated on maintaining its own balance, the system rests on the authority of the elders and the solidarity of all members of the community.... The factors involved in rural development are not mainly of a technical nature but depend on political, social and economic structures to which the agricultural worker's destiny is closely tied [148, p. 12-13].

---

1. Opening address at the World Conference on Agricultural Education and Training, Copenhagen, 1970.

There are increasingly widening gaps between the cities and the countryside, replicating the imbalances and injustices which, in a general way, characterize the relations between industrialized areas and underdeveloped areas.

In most countries, the governments have a tendency, for many reasons, to concentrate most of their development efforts on urban areas to the detriment of the rural communities [119f, p. 247; 99, p. 79]. In the cities, the average incomes are often many times greater than the average farmer's income. Is it at all surprising that, under these conditions, the cities act like huge magnets, attracting the rural inhabitants and especially the young people who have been to school? To become a city-dweller then becomes a synonym for promotion in the social scale.

The dangers of this trend are obvious: shanty towns, massive unemployment, social disturbances, etc.[1] One of its most serious effects is that it is first the most dynamic and best educated elements who desert the countryside. In the developed countries, where agriculture is well on the way to being industrialized, these problems are perhaps less acute; but to admit that they do not exist or have been solved would be an illusion. There too, the structures and subject-matter of education, in their present form, conform primarily to the socio-economic and cultural requirements of the urban populations.

Requirements and priorities for agricultural development

The precariousness of the world food situation is well known. According to a document of the World Food Conference held in 1974, approximately 460 million people in the world were suffering from serious nutritional deficiencies in 1970, and sixty-one out of ninety-seven developing countries showed a food deficit. The disasters which have recently swept the Sahel and certain Asian countries are a tragic illustration of the reality of the danger which is threatening the very lives of their populations [99, p. 76]. Recent events have shown that the industrialized countries can also experience difficulties in supplying themselves with sufficient food.

To increase agricultural productivity is the only means of solving the problem of hunger and preventing a world food catastrophe. The

1. 'The recent movements of students are nothing, in my opinion, in comparison to what could happen when the unemployed intellectuals take the leadership of the medinas of Africa,' Joseph KI-ZERBO [119d, p. 417].

fact that the developing countries alone have some 60 million new mouths to feed every year goes to prove the urgency of the problem.

Agricultural development is an indispensable factor, and often the driving force, in any over-all process of economic development. For the developing countries, the exportation of agricultural products is by far the most important source of foreign exchange which will enable them to buy the capital goods needed for modernizing their economies. In addition, agricultural development, among other things, contributes to the process of industrialization, either by supplying raw materials to farm and food industries or through purchases of industrial goods which stimulate industrial growth [84, p. 64].

The rural sector, therefore, which has been relatively neglected in the past, deserves special attention. Depending on numerous and interdependent social and economic factors, this sector should be the object of what is called by general agreement 'integrated planning'— a new and pivotal idea of development.

Rural development and the increase of productivity are, to a large extent, a matter of improving agricultural techniques: the introduction of new methods of cultivation, new seeds, the use of fertilizers and agricultural machinery, the improvement of such infrastructures as irrigation systems, etc.

However, all these techniques require knowledge and practical know-how. The development of agriculture calls for farmers, both men and women, who are better educated, better trained, more dynamic, who can understand the needs of their particular locality and adjust themselves to changes. In the most backward rural areas, what must be done first of all is to overcome lethargy and stagnation.[1] For there is no development except where there is change, and there is no change except where there is movement.

The development of attitudes and aptitudes is an indispensable condition for the growth of the agricultural sector and for improving the quality of life of rural populations. This is, therefore, an educational problem of the greatest importance. For this reason, it is not surprising that the senior officials of the ministries of education of the countries of Latin America and the Caribbean, meeting in Panama City in February 1976, noted 'the unprecedented concern and attention which is beginning to be given to the education of the population of rural areas' [87, p. 13].

---

1. 'Education should serve as a force to rouse them from their state of passive *being* and set them on the path on *becoming*' [69, p. 4].

Nevertheless, we should still remain aware of the fact that education is, in any circumstances, an indispensable tool, although not in itself a sufficient one, for giving rise to processes of change and socio-economic development.

Education never produces miracles. In the context of development, its effects depend to a large extent on how fully it is integrated with all other measures taken to trigger or accelerate the process of economic and social development.

Educational underdevelopment in rural areas

'The vast, sombre areas of the planet which constitute the geography of ignorance [are primarily agricultural],' says Edgar Faure, Chairman of the International Committee for the Development of Education [54, p. xxi].

'Throughout the world, it is in rural areas that the short-comings of modern education are most serious,' says Mr. A.-M. M'Bow, Director-General of Unesco [87, p. 74]. 'Inadequate educational services for rural areas could have truly catastrophic results,' as we are warned by L. Malassis, one of the best experts in this field [84, p. 17].

The rural areas of the developing countries are the zones with the lowest rates of school attendance and, consequently, with the highest rates of illiteracy. To this must be added the fact that nowhere else does school wastage achieve rates that could be more disastrous.

Let us just try to sketch, in a few broad strokes, a typical school in one of the large agricultural areas where poverty and misery endure. The school is situated in any place which comes to hand. It has practically no teaching facilities. The teacher himself, who faces an enormous class of 100 pupils and more, all of different ages, has a training which is completely inadequate. More often than not he has not gone farther than primary education.[1] He is badly paid. The pupils come from illiterate backgrounds which are unable to support their learning in any way. They suffer from malnutrition, which tends to lower their interest and mental ability. They are often sick, suffering from malaria or victims of parasites. Many of them have had to walk for several hours in order to get to school.

---

1. In the United Republic of Cameroon, in 1970, to cite only this example among many others, 72.2 per cent of the teachers were monitors whose only diploma was their certificate for having completed their primary studies [79, p. 16].

'In many African, Latin American and Asian countries, more than half the pupils of primary schools, particularly in rural areas, drop out entirely after the second year' [148, p. 17]. They will therefore relapse into illiteracy like all those who have attended school for less than three years.

The education provided in the rural schools of the Third World (and elsewhere) is often poorly adapted to the needs of agricultural populations.[1] In Africa in particular, where it is still largely conditioned by the heritage of the colonial past, education is still often too 'literary', and primarily intended to train auxiliary officials. This is a kind of education, then, which for all practical purposes leads nowhere.

Instead of being a powerful instrument of social, economic and cultural progress, the village school in the Third World, which is badly adapted to its purpose, educationally underdeveloped, poorly equipped and inefficiently managed, frequently becomes a factor of underdevelopment and contributes to the flight from the land.[2] It is then a bad thing rather than a good one.

In view of all these deficiencies and difficulties, one can understand that, to a certain extent, governments and 'most of the planning bodies at the central level customarily neglect the area of rural education'[3] in favour of higher education, and also sometimes in favour of prestige projects.[4] Fortunately, it is possible to perceive a reversal of this situation, particularly in Latin America, Asia and some African countries.

The ruralization of education

Up to relatively recent times, the 'ruralization' of education was understood as meaning the injection of a few elements of agricultural

1. A description of the most relevant deficiencies in education in some developing countries has been made by Joseph KI-ZERBO. We warmly recommend reading his article 'Education and development' [119d, p. 410-29 and 159, p. 94-113].

2. Joseph KI-ZERBO writes: 'The school in many underdeveloped countries is a reflection and a fruit of the surrounding underdevelopment, from which arises its deficiency, its quantitative and qualitative poverty. But little by little—and there lies the really serious risk—the school in these underdeveloped countries risks becoming in turn a factor of underdevelopment' [119d, p. 411].

3. See: Takeshi MOTOOKA, 'Education for rural development: investments in developing countries' [119f, p. 239-45].

4. 'Almost all less-developed countries suffer from persistent under-investment in primary education, hand-in-hand with persistent over-investment in higher education'. Mark BLAUG, 'Economics and educational planning in developing countries' [119d, p. 431].

training into the curricula of schools in the country: in botany, the study of various species of cereals and vegetables; in zoology, the study of cattle, sheep, goats and rats; in arithmetic, bags of potatoes were multiplied by the dozen; and, in particular, a certain amount of gardening was done.

Today, 'ruralization' is understood as meaning all measures taken to adapt education systems to the needs of rural populations. 'In the view of the UNC Party and the Government, ruralization means the adaptation of education to the actual conditions of this country, which is essentially agricultural,' said, for example, His Excellency El Adj Ahmadou Ahidjo, President of the United Republic of Cameroon when awarding diplomas to the students of the Institute of Rurally Oriented Applied Education (IPAR) in 1970 [79, p. 43].

Such measures may be of a material nature. First of all, what has to be done is to build more schools in rural areas. Few facts are available to us in this field, since the statistics on the quantitative expansion of education seldom give any indices about developments in rural areas. However, a certain number of countries were sufficiently aware of the problem to give some indications in the reports they presented to the thirty-fifth session of the International Conference on Education. We might mention, among others, the USSR, where a decree of the Central Committee of the Communist Party and the Council of Ministers provides for the construction in rural areas of new school buildings having a total capacity of 9.26 million pupils. When carried out, this decree will make it possible to build one general secondary school in every *sovkhoz* and every large *kolkhoz*.[1] In Poland, the school network, which had hitherto been rather widely dispersed over the countryside, has been concentrated in collective communal schools. These schools include nursery schools, primary schools, elementary vocational schools for agricultural training, elementary agricultural schools, secondary general schools and secondary vocational schools. A special effort is being made to create pre-school educational institutions in the country. At present, the number of children in nursery schools and pre-school centres is increasing twice as fast in the countryside as in the cities. In Peru and in other Latin American countries, hundreds of *nucleos educativos comunales* have been established (see p. 160). In Pakistan, it is planned to increase the

---

1. USSR. Central Committee of the CPSU and the Council of Ministers of the USSR. 'Measures for further improvement of working conditions in the rural general school.' *Pravda* (Moskva), 7 July 1973.

standard of 3,630 primary schools and 1,480 intermediate schools in rural areas. Other countries, such as Iraq,[1] the Philippines, Tunisia and Turkey are making special efforts to improve the rate of school attendance of children in rural areas.

Other measures have also been introduced to enable more rural children to attend school, such as the organization of transport facilities for them and the establishment of canteens and boarding schools. In Algeria, boarding schools have been established for the elementary education of nomadic children in the Saharan areas. In that same country, 882,000 pupils were using school canteens in 1975. Another Maghreb country, Tunisia, has also established many canteens for students in rural areas. In addition, it is organizing methods of transporting the students to the country schools. In the USSR, the decree mentioned above provides for the organization of regular, free modes of transport for pupils from their homes to and from school. This may be by bus, train, river boat or other facilities set up especially by the *kolkhozes, sovkhozes* and various other enterprises and organizations.

In the hilly parts of China, where the pupils are widely scattered, it is the teachers who move around to give their lessons. Water-borne schools have been opened for the children of fishermen [119o, p. 485]. In Cuba, itinerant services have also been created for the benefit of small rural schools. In Saudi Arabia, the teachers travel around by helicopter with their school equipment, while in the Libyan Arab Jamahiriya, mobile prefabricated classrooms are used on a relatively large scale to facilitate teaching in remote areas.

Some countries think that they can make up for educational deficiencies in rural areas by decentralizing their administrative structures. For example, in Iran, decentralization of the education system has had the result that planning today is carried out by regional education boards and the plans are adapted to the special needs and conditions of the various parts of the country.[2] Pakistan and Indonesia have carried out a similar decentralization of planning. Comparable changes have been made in Singapore's system of educational administration and management [122, p. 9], and in the Congo.

---

1. In Iraq, the rate of school attendance in rural areas rose from 48.3 per cent in 1972/73 to 57.2 per cent in 1973/74.
2. See: Iraj AYMAN, *Educational innovation in Iran* [3].

A particularly interesting and significant reform in this field is being carried out in Peru, with its 'nuclear systems' (*nucleos educativos comunales* or NEC).[1] All the local institutions responsible for the various educational needs of the community are grouped around a *centro base* (usually a secondary school) which directs and co-ordinates the activities of the NEC: basic education for young people and adults (*educación básica regular* and *educación básica laboral*), secondary education, vocational training, adult literacy classes, cultural activities, etc. The NEC include all the installations which meet these needs: schools, libraries, workshops, laboratories, sport fields, etc. The NEC are closely linked to all aspects of community life. They enjoy a very large degree of autonomy, since they are managed by *Consejos educativos comunales* (composed of teachers, parents and representatives of the communal authorities and various local groups, such as trade unions, etc.). What this amounts to, therefore, is a real transfer of power in the field of education and a real participation by the community in educational management. The 819 NECs in the country, which constitute the basic units of the entire Peruvian education system, are grouped into twenty-eight zones, which in turn form nine areas.

There appears to be a different trend in Poland. In this country, the small rural schools are being concentrated into larger and better equipped establishments, since the rural school network was considered too widely scattered. However, these collective communal schools, which comprise nursery schools, primary schools, elementary vocational and agricultural preparatory schools, elementary agricultural schools, secondary general schools and secondary vocational schools, are independent units at the administrative and budgetary level.

In some Arab countries, villages which are too small to justify a school are reorganized for the same purpose, and efforts are made to persuade nomads to become sedentary.

Problems of centralization, decentralization and co-ordination also arise at another level, that of governmental structures. In many countries, different ministries are responsible for different aspects of education in rural areas.[2] This leads to obvious difficulties. This is why there is an increased tendency to make rural education, in all its

---

1. See: Judithe BIZOT, *Educational reform in Peru* [9] and Peru's report to the thirty-fifth session of the International Conference on Education.
2. See: Takeshi MOTOOKA, 'Education for rural development: investment in developing countries' [119f, p. 239-45, particularly p. 240].

forms, the exclusive responsibility of the ministries of education, or at least to create bodies for inter-ministerial co-ordination.

There is no publication and no report concerning education in rural areas which does not emphasize the shortage of teachers, and especially adequately qualified teachers. Teachers are attracted by the cities, where they are better paid, where they feel less isolated, where living and working conditions are better, and where the schools are better equipped. In this way, the differences between the cities and the rural areas become even more pronounced—another cause of the flight from the land.

However, although these facts are very widely recognized, it must be noted that very few countries ever draw the logical conclusions from them. Almost everywhere, the political pressures exerted on governments by urban populations are stronger than those exerted by the farmers, who often do not have the necessary means of making themselves heard and who live far away from the decision-making centres.

In some countries, teacher training schools have been established which provide a shorter and less academic training in order to attract young peasants to the teaching profession who will be able to do their work in a familiar environment [20, p. 63]. And yet it is the rural teachers who should receive special additional training, since they ought to be both school-teachers and effective community development leaders in the villages [121, p. 46].

Among the few countries which base the ruralization of their education on teacher training designed for that purpose is the United Republic of Cameroon, whose Institute of Rurally Oriented Applied Education (IPAR) prepares teachers for their multiple functions in the new 'ruralized' schools.[1] A teacher training reform along the same lines is being carried out in Liberia.

In some countries, such as the USSR for example, certain privileges are granted to teachers in rural areas. In other countries, they have to serve for a period of time in a rural area before they can be promoted.

The most important aspect of the ruralization of education is probably the adaptation of teaching and its subject-matter to the needs of rural societies.

---

1. See: Raymond LALLEZ, *An experiment in the ruralization of education: IPAR and the Cameroonian reform* [79].

To educate is to make every man the depository of all the works of men before him, an up-to-date epitome of the living world; it is to raise him to the level of his era so that he can stay on top of it and not to leave him below the level of his age where he can never get on top; it is to prepare the individual for life. . . .

Divorcing man from the soil is a monstrous crime. It is the simplest of analogies: for the birds, wings; for the fish, fins; for Man living in the midst of nature, knowledge of nature—which represents his wings. And the only means of giving him his wings is to make the scientific element as it were the back-bone of the system of public education; let science teaching, like the sap in the trees, run from the roots to the summit of public education. Let elementary education have its meed of elementary science. . . .

An error of the utmost gravity is being committed in Latin America: in nations living almost entirely off the products of the countryside, the education given is exclusively for life in cities, with no preparation for the life of the field. . . to study modern agriculture in the prosperous farmlands; to pass a harvest or harvests living in the farms. . . .

Physical, mental and moral benefits come from manual work. . . . Man grows with the work of his hands. . . and behind each school an agricultural workshop opened in rain and sun where each student may plant a tree. . . it is not dry pages of mere printed line, which bring forth the fruits of life. . . .

Here as everywhere the problem consists in planting the seed. The teaching of agriculture is more urgent that ever but. . . in agricultural stations where they do not describe the parts of the plough but show them on the plough and handle the plough; and the composition of the soil is not explained by blackboard formulae but in the actual fields.

. . . Whereas the man who owes his well-being to his work or has filled his life with the creation and transformation of forces and the exercise of his own energies is bright-eyed, vivid of speech and steady of hand. Obviously it is these last who make the world.

There is only one magic wand at whose stroke all rocks yield springs of water: it is work.

The term schools should not be used, but workshops; the pen should be used there in the afternoon, but in the morning the hoe.

José MARTI (1853-95)
Poet, thinker and Cuban patriot [55, p. 2-3].

The rural world needs young people who are:

1. Dynamic, capable of adapting themselves to change and especially to agricultural progress, fond of farm work and able to use their hands;
2. Ready to participate in the development of their community;
3. Capable of providing for a family and raising children;
4. Persons having an elementary knowledge of natural processes and an understanding of agricultural tools and machinery;
5. Persons who know how to read, write and calculate.

It is obvious that, in actual practice, these needs will vary, depending on the cultural context, the level of development and the natural environment of the society in question. The ruralization of the subject-matter of education, therefore, means much more than the introduction of a few elements of agricultural training into school programmes. These ideas are reflected in educational reforms and experiments in rural countries.

In this connexion, the Cuban system of basic secondary schools in the country (*escuelas secondarias básicas en el campo*), going from the seventh to the tenth school year, is of particular interest.[1] These schools are based on the principle of a combination of study and farm work. Each of them is built for 500 pupils (250 boys and 250 girls), and 200 hectares of land are assigned to them for cultivation. The pupils live in the school during the five working days of the week. The fundamental educational principle which governs all education in Cuba is that work, and productive work first of all, is in itself a powerful factor for developing the personality. In the secondary schools in the country, training is closely linked to productive work. The pupils work every day in the school plantations, the rest of the time being reserved for their lessons (four and a half hours in the classroom and a two hours' study period) and for cultural activities and sports (one hour). One day per week, the pupils have a free evening after 17.30. A collective mentality prevails in all activities; individualism and egoism are systematically opposed. The Cuban system not only has an educational foundation, but also an economic background. Considering that Cuba is a poor country, the Govern-

---

1. Max FIGUEROA; Abel PRIETO; Raoul GUTIERREZ, *The basic secondary school in the country: an educational innovation in Cuba* [55] and Max FIGUEROA ARAUJO, 'The Cuban school in the countryside' [119p, p. 129-31].

ment takes the view that only an education system combining teaching with productive activities can supply the State with the necessary resources which will enable it to provide universal secondary education.

Cuba is not the only country where education is combined with agricultural production and where the productive work of the pupils helps to finance the school. In the Congo, experiments are underway for the establishment of rural schools which will be entirely self-sufficient. In Benin, educational reform provides that every school establishment should be organized as a school co-operative and should also double as a production unit. Chad is working along similar lines. In Ethiopia, it is planned that every school in rural areas should possess ten hectares of land and should, if necessary, be self-sufficient. Similar systems are also found in China.

In the USSR, the pupils take part in the work in the fields in school brigades. There are also farm learning centres: these combine studies with production. And also agricultural learning centres: these combine studies with production and provide training for the various agricultural trades.

Other countries do not go as far as the few examples given above and confine themselves to including a few agricultural subjects in their courses, without aiming at any actual production.

In December 1975, a Regional Seminar on Quality in the Educational Process: Education and Social and Economic Development in Africa was held at Lomé, Togo. In the working document proposed for this meeting, Robert Mélet, the Unesco consultant, attacked the 'mistake and failure' of the 'ruralization' of education [134, p. 1]. His was by far not the only critical voice. Many authors before him, particularly Louis Malassis [84 and 119f, p. 219-30], have denounced the 'pitfalls of ruralization'.

There is a danger with education adapted to the rural environment, especially at the primary level, that it may become a cut-price or unilateral education, that it may again discriminate against young rural inhabitants in favour of city-dwellers, that it may help to widen still farther the gap between urban and farming populations. There is also the danger that ruralization may lead young people up a blind alley, a ghetto, by blocking to even the most intelligent among them access to higher levels of education. In that way, instead of helping to solve the problems of rural inhabitants, instead of remedying injustices, instead of stopping the flight from the land, the school would only serve to emphasize social inequalities, with all their consequences.

Today, the great majority of responsible educators are aware of these dangers. At many intergovernmental meetings, they state that there should not be two types of education—one for rural areas and the other for urban areas. Certain major educational reforms are explicitly based on this principle. In the United Republic of Cameroon, to cite only one example, the Head of State declared: 'When I refer to the ruralization of education, I do not mean a cut-price education for peasant's children' [79, p. 43]. Other official texts do not hesitate to carry this idea further: 'The rural primary school will be the only primary school, whether in town or country. It will be attended by all children, both those going on to the secondary school and those who will embark immediately upon their working life on leaving school' [79, p. 29].

However, the problem is still a complex one. How can we persuade young people to become farmers if farming conditions are such that their principal characteristic is material and intellectual poverty, and if farming offers practically no chance of personal fulfilment and social advancement? [1] In these conditions, how can we stop young people from leaving the land, and especially those young people who are dynamic and have received a certain education, without forcing them, or without barring their way somehow or other to the false promises held out by the cities? And as the same time, how can we discover the intelligent minds which these countries need to ensure their development, and how can we lead them on to secondary education, not to mention higher education? How can we prevent marginalization and halt the trend towards the reduction of the rural world to a proletarian status? Concerning this subject, Louis Malassis writes: 'The problems of rural development cannot be solved by educational segregation: only when agriculture itself is transformed will rural education begin to take on its real significance' [84, p. 22].

Once again we find ourselves confronted with the problem of integrated development, of which education is only one element—an important one, it is true—among others. Mr. Majid Rahnema, the Iranian member of Unesco's Executive Board, said the following in May 1976 at a Board meeting:

---

1. The question also arises in countries where agriculture is in the process of industrialization. 'Research in France has shown that 90 to 100 per cent of young people who study beyond the minimum school-leaving age do not return to family farming' [137, p. 4].

How is it conceivable that we can open up new methods for integrated rural development and, alternatively, prevent the dangerous trends towards the 'ruralization' of education or the encouragement of a cut-price education for the rural masses, if these ways do not include a whole number of measures aimed at all the socio-economic, cultural, ecological or other factors, including the school, which are causing the deterioration of life and, in village communities, their deculturation and the flight to the cities of the products of the school? No, it is no longer possible to envisage serious reforms in no matter what field of education ... without envisaging these reforms as a systematic whole in which everything is interconnected and everything holds together. Education, like the development with which it is integrated, is a symmetrical pattern in which it is impossible to change one part without altering the whole.

The role of out-of-school education

Wherever only a part of the young people—and often only a small minority—attend school,[1] and where, moreover, a large number of the pupils stay in school for such a short length of time that it is barely enough to teach them how to read and write, it is necessary to look for other ways to develop abilities and transmit the knowledge and practical intelligence which constitute the 'minimum package' enabling young people to assume the full responsibilities of adulthood.[2]

Some think that in rural areas non-formal education is the ideal way to make up for the deficits and deficiencies or mistakes of the school. For this reason, many agricultural countries are endeavouring to develop the out-of-school sectors of their education systems. The list of non-formal programmes offered in Kenya is an example of this (see pages 168-9).

The rural polytechnic school in Kenya, which is included in this inventory, offers an especially attractive formula. This is a centre for learning rural trades—agriculture, stock-raising, bee-keeping, masonry, carpentry, plumbing, sewing, baking, etc.—which operates

---

1. In countries with a low rate of school attendance, there are often very great disparities between urban areas and rural areas. 'For example, in Upper Volta it is said that 9 per cent of the children in the whole country go to school, but this percentage varies from 40 per cent at Ouagadougou and 33 per cent at Bobo to 4 per cent at Kaya and 3 per cent at Titao' [119d, p. 464].

2. See p. 139, as well as our section giving examples of the objectives of education, p. 17. Concerning rural education, such authors as Philip H. COOMBS, [28, p. 13-17; 119g, p. 319-22] and Louis MALASSIS [84, p. 89] have provided some indications of this 'minimum package'.

at a low cost and is designed to meet the needs of pupils who are leaving primary education. It does not award any diplomas, but merely teaches people to do a job. In most cases, the teachers are recruited among artisans in the locality. These centres are mainly administered by the local communities. It is planned to establish 250 rural polytechnics for 22,500 pupils between now and the end of 1978.[1]

Another example is the Jombang project in Indonesia. This is due to the initiative of the *Bupati* (chief of the Regency) of Kabupaten, a former police officer. With the help of boy scouts in the rural areas, representatives of the various co-operatives and the heads of the departments of agriculture, education, irrigation, stock-raising, fisheries and health, he plans to establish various learning programmes for young people in some of the villages of his Regency, combined with paid activities. Whole villages are participating actively in these projects.[2]

Among the number of unsolved problems which continue to be an object of concern in educational circles, we shall mention here only two more which seem to us to be particularly important. One is the problem of co-ordination between the school and the many non-formal activities and, furthermore, the integration of the various educational approaches in a coherent and over-all system which should, in turn, be part of a system of activities aimed at development. The other problem is that of the limited number of people involved, even in those activities which seem to be among the most successful. Often there are only a few hundred of them—and, moreover, they are almost exclusively people who have already had a school education. In this connexion, literacy campaigns (see p. 66) are an exception.

The birth of new types of educational institutions

It must never be forgotten that the traditional societies—which were all agricultural societies—perhaps lacked schools but did not lack education. (The school is a relatively recent European invention.) Everywhere in the world there have always been procedures for training young people and transmitting to them the knowledge possessed by society which they needed to assume their role and responsibilities

1. See: E.A. WANJALA, 'The village polytechnic movement in Kenya' [119n, p. 440-4], and Philip H. COOMBS [28, p. 46 and 26, p. 146].
2. See: *Educational innovation in Indonesia* [70, p. 35-9].

KENYA

Inventory of non-formal education programmes

I. Government.

   A. *Department of Community Development and Social Services:*

      1. Youth clubs and centres (usually run by local government or voluntary bodies);

      2. Village Polytechnics (run by Christian Council of Kenya);

      3. Community Development Training Centres (run by local governments);

      4. Community Development self-help movement (with non-formal education function);

      5. Literacy classes (government and voluntary agencies);

      6. Two co-ordinating organizations: Board of Adult Education and National Youth Council.

   B. *Ministry of Agriculture:*

      1. 4-K movement;

      2. Farmer Training Centres.

   C. *Ministry of Labour:*

      1. National Youth Service;

      2. Vocational Training Centres.

   D. *Ministry of Health*

      1. Health Centres (with local governments; instructional programmes for girls and women);

   E. *Ministry of Education:*

      1. Equivalence courses (post-primary) with university, and using radio-correspondence.

   F. *Ministry of Information:*

      1. Instructional radio;

      3. Instructional television;

      3. Information and civic publications.

II. Non-government.

   A. *Churches* (including Protestant denominations, Catholic Muslim):

      1. Village Polytechnics (Protestant and Catholic);

      2. Vocational training;

      3. Rural Training Centres.

   B. *Boy Scouts.*

   C. *Girl Guides.*

   D. *YMCA.*

   E. *YWCA.*

   F. *Red Cross.*

   G. *Maendeleo ya Wanawake* ('Progress for Women')— women's movement with an educational function.

   H. *Various tribal associations* (some have educational programmes).

III. Quasi-government.

   A. *University:*

      1. Adult education classes;

      2. Undergraduate voluntary service groups.

   B. *Local governments*

      1. Staffing and support especially for community development training centres, health centres, and community development movement.

Source: Philip H. COOMBS, *New paths to learning for rural children and youth* [28, p. 105-6].

as adults. The most significant were the initiation rites. The whole village participated in educating the young. The village was the school.

Today, one can observe trends towards a new symbiosis between the school and the village. In some countries, especially rural countries, the school is less and less regarded as a closed-off area where a person passes a certain part of his youth acquiring certain very specific kinds of knowledge—which often have nothing to do with everyday life.

The school is now bursting wide open and addressing itself to adults as well as to young people, sometimes to both at the same time; it is stimulating and waking up the village; it is becoming the meeting-place of the village, the village focal point; it is managed by the village and contributes to the work of the village.

This trend is very clearly apparent in the educational reform carried out in the United Republic of Cameroon [79], where the new village school is a centre for encouragement and persuasion and where the teacher is trained to be both teacher and group leader. There, the 'ruralized' primary school becomes the springboard for collective advancement. The official texts about this reform are unambiguous:

> The willingness of adults to set to work to transform their present ways of life will be greatly facilitated if the village has before it the model supplied by the school (poultry yard, garden, plantation, canteen, latrines, pure well water). The adults will gradually imitate the school if the latter provides practical examples for transforming the environment which will satisfy their needs for profit, health and recreation. ... The results [of the work of the teacher-group leader] will gradually stimulate and encourage the adolescent and adult strata of the population; the school will become a centre of persuasion and the teacher, esteemed by the inhabitants, will be asked to direct and organize the adults' efforts to achieve a better way of life [84, p. 78 ff.].

In the United Republic of Tanzania, a pilot project has been started at Kwamisi which is aimed at the complete integration of school life with that of the inhabitants. 'The result is a general feeling of solidarity', and, consequently, a pooling of all resources and all efforts for the success of the community as a whole. Henceforth the school is a part of this community, as confirmed by the fact that, with respect to administrative matters, the chairman of the village directs the village as a whole, including the school [21e, p. 20].

In the Philippines, the experiment with the 'barrios schools', i.e. secondary village schools, has shown how a co-operative approach could overcome economic obstacles, while renewing the school system at the same time. The rural community is responsible for these schools, the number of which increased from four in 1965 to 1,700 in 1973.[1] *All* the persons in question—pupils, parents, teachers and all others—were involved in one way or another in launching the project, defining its objectives, planning strategies or methods of approach, evaluating the results and subsequently revising the programme. Experts in Manila or elsewhere were not consulted about what to do and how to do it, but the best possible use was made of the local resources—teachers, parents who became part-time teachers, grandmothers who told the children stories of former times, local leaders, etc. The teachers compared their experiences and drew up new directives aimed at improving their teaching; they subsequently applied these directives and revised them when necessary.

No expensive equipment was acquired, either materials were improvised or those materials available were used. This was for two reasons. The first was one of economy: instead of buying PL.500 worth of science teaching aids per school, which no school could afford, the pupils improvised their own equipment themselves by using reconditioned articles. The second reason was to make the subject-matter of the teaching—i.e. the sciences—more interesting and stimulating for the students.

Use was made of 'foreign experience', at least that which was known about, by adapting it to local needs and problems and making necessary changes here and there. It was not assumed that all the innovations were necessarily good, or that all the traditional or old-fashioned methods were bad. In all cases, the people decided, after a discussion, what they wanted to do and how they wanted it to be done. They were left to feel their way just as the group leaders had felt their way, and to discover their own mistakes so that they could correct them all the better (and in this way educate themselves).

In India, experimental schools have been established where the entire community can come to receive instruction, and in Latin America similar examples are found in Colombia, Honduras, Mexico, etc.

In his book *Education in Africa, what next ?* [92], Dragoljub Najman has imagined a new kind of school.

---

1. The whole of this next passage is based on the book by the group leader of this project: Pedrot ORATA, *Self-help barrio high schools*. Singapore, Eastern University Press, 1972, p. 16.

My idea is a school, or rather an institution, which would give basic knowledge and skills to both children and parents in a rural community. Whether this education should be given to both age groups simultaneously or not remains a question of practical solutions. I would favour education given to groups of parents and children jointly, so that they would study together under the leadership of someone who would be both a teacher and a kind of community leader.

This community school would deliver basic education to youngsters and elders at the same time. Instead of grades and classes and examinations to pass, an institution like this might have an initial course and an advanced course. Both children and elders could remain in this institution for a certain number of years until they had achieved what some people call the 'terminal performance specifications'.

The time spent at school would be adapted to the needs of the rural economy, and obviously both children and elders could go to school at a time of day and at a time of year when they are not required to work in the fields.... For some years to come, most of those attending this new institution would remain in the village and work for the rural economy, but both elders, and especially young people who have shown particular ability, would be sent to special transitional classes enabling them to continue their education in more formal institutions at the secondary, technical or higher levels. The important thing for the new institution would be that education and instruction would not be imposed by outsiders, who had decided what and how they should be taught, nor by means of rigid curricula, at fixed hours and on fixed days. Education would be a mutual process whereby the group of youngsters and elders, together with the teacher, would try to find the best answers to questions posed. In this system there would be a real integration between instruction and education, between school and out-of-school education, between the education of young people and adult education. Education would become one of the normal activities for everybody in the village and not, as is the case at present, a separate activity for a very few fortunate ones who learn strange and foreign things [92, p. 61-2].

EDUCATION AND CULTURE

'For us today in Africa, every form of development must proceed from culture and find its ultimate meaning in culture. It is culture, therefore, which is the great inspiring force and it is culture, in fact, which will be the ultimate achievement', says the Togolese sociologist and diplomat, N'Sougan Agblemagnon.[1]

1. N'Sougan AGBLEMAGNON, *Buts et finalités de l'éducation en Afrique*, a report presented at the second meeting of Unesco consultants on 'Goals and theories of education', Paris, June 1976.

This is not the place to engage in the interminable—although extremely interesting—debate about the idea of 'culture' and its many definitions. It is obvious that in talks about this subject, different acceptations and definitions of the term are constantly being confused. And, very often, divergences of opinion on this subject are due merely to the fact that the speakers are not talking about the same thing. Moreover, it seems obvious that the dazzling notion of culture cannot be expressed in one simple definition, any more than it is possible to express in a few sentences what a human being is or the meaning of human existence.

Today, in principle, it is possible to distinguish two conceptions. The traditional one understands by the term 'culture' everything relating to the 'world of the mind': philosophical thought, literature, the fine arts, music, the theatre, etc.; the other, more modern and much broader conception, that of the anthropologists, refers to culture as 'the sum-total of values, institutions and ways of behaviour which are transmitted collectively within a society, as well as the material goods produced by man'. [1]

The cultural field, therefore, lies between the relatively precise boundaries of 'literature and the fine arts' and the indeterminate middle ground of the 'material goods created by man'. It is characterized by such notions as 'values' or 'significance', while the objects created by man—and sometimes even natural objects—become 'cultural' in so far as some meaning is given to them, i.e. if they are connected with a system of values and meanings.

Every human society has its counterpart in a cultural system which it has secreted. Formerly, one used to talk about the 'soul of the nation', but today it is rather its cultural identity, the unifying idea of populations, nations and even regions. Myths, religions, various kinds of knowledge and above all languages are, among other things, fundamental components of every culture.

To be a creator of cultures is an essential characteristic of mankind. Man is the sole creator of cultures. It is in culture that he fulfils himself.

Culture and education are closely linked. They are two facets of one and the same reality. It is impossible to determine where the educational one leaves off and the cultural one begins. And it would be absurd to try to separate them.

---

1. Roy PREISWERK, *Relations interculturelles et développement* [71, p. 16].

Among the cultural functions of education, we might point out that it is education which transmits culture from generation to generation, and that it is also education which opens the way to culture. Or, as Bertrand Schwartz says, 'This cultural need... is the product of education.... The educational system is directly involved in achieving universal participation in cultural life' [131, p. 26]. It is through education that young people are introduced to and made a part of the culture of adults. However, if the school becomes a special society within society and cut off from it, it begins to produce its own culture, a counter-culture of young people and adolescents who rebel against the culture of the adults.[1]

The educational role of culture is also a multiple one; it is from culture that the fundamental trends of education—and of life—are derived. To listen to music, visit a museum or art gallery, read a novel, attend a play, are all educational acts as well as forms of participation in culture. They are also forms of learning. A visit to a museum is often as educational as a lesson in history or geography.

It would be easy to multiply these examples. We might merely add that to develop an individual's creativity—the special importance of which in a changing world has been emphasized several times in this book—is an activity about which it is impossible to say whether it is educational or cultural.

At the present time, it is not just by chance that the same problems are arising with regard to culture as with regard to education: access to culture, the democratization of culture, are the great subjects of modern cultural policy. The 'educational city' has its counterpart in 'cultural democracy'. Lifelong education and cultural development aim in a similar way at the full development of the personality. Today more than ever, education and culture are intermingling. It is significant that the Council of Europe, whose role in encouraging the development of the lifelong education concept we have already referred to, has defined one of its main objectives in its medium-term plan, 1976-80, as follows: 'Fostering increasing interaction between cultural development and permanent education policies' [30, p. 27].

These considerations are far from being purely philosophical or theoretical. For some practical questions arise in this context, such as, for example: how can we use such cultural institutions as museums,

1. Concerning this, see: Jean-Marie DOMENACH. 'Education and society in the context of the Western industrialized countries' [119p, p. 7-18].

libraries, theatres, cinemas, art collections and orchestras with due regard for the criteria, methods and objectives of lifelong education? How can we open up the world of culture in education; how can we teach people to look at a picture, to decipher a work of art or the meaning of a ritual object; how can we develop aesthetic sensibility and the joy of creating (or how can we prevent the school from destroying the child's creative gifts)?

The solution of these problems is often made difficult by the fact that, in many States, the same administrative structures are not responsible for the fields of both education and culture. On the one hand, ministries of education usually confine themselves to administering schools, i.e. academic institutions only; while on the other hand, ministries of culture restrict themselves to preserving the country's cultural heritage, administering or subsidizing the major traditional cultural institutions and granting some assistance to artistic creation. As in other fields, integration of the different policies is becoming more and more urgent, and especially so, in the case before us, in the so-called 'developed' countries.

In the preceding chapters, however, there are several examples—such as the comprehensive community centres, etc.—which show how the problem of much closer liaison between cultural activities and education might be solved in practice.

Education systems are an essential component of all the various cultures. Serious problems arise wherever the education system is a foreign body, either because it has been imposed or imported and not secreted by the society in question or because it is the inherited residue of a former society. Two cultural models then confront each other, and in a particularly sensitive field. This is the case in the great majority of developing countries. Africa is perhaps the region where this problem is felt most acutely. This continent would seem to be the one which has been most strongly affected in this field by the trauma of colonization. It still bears deep and angry scars from this experience. This is why it is so intent on finding its own real character, its own cultural identity, as well as education systems which are genuinely African.

The search for authentic cultural sources from which to derive firm guidelines for renewing education or, better still, for creating truly relevant education systems, is one of the most striking trends in the present history of education. Efforts aimed at combining traditional forms of education with the needs of the present age— 'reinvesting the traditional cultural capital in modern education'

[86a, p. 18]—have an extremely promising future and without doubt will greatly influence the development of education systems, especially in the Third World.

It is also fascinating to note the extent to which the most advanced theories about an education open to its surroundings and the community are harking back to ancient traditions in which education, work and culture used to constitute a whole. The traditional society lived in an atmosphere in which human life was a unity—a harmony of work and religion. 'Culture' and education did not become separated from that unity until relatively recent times.

It is necessary, of course, to avoid false romanticism. At one seminar, certain delegates from East African countries rightly stated the following:

> However, warning voices are raised against being carried away by a nostalgic, exclusively anthropological view of the past, and against believing too readily that values and attitudes have not already been fundamentally changed by the impingement of modern socio-economic mores in even the most remote areas. Perhaps a 'hotch-potch' of cultures is already in existence—or a 'dualism' which is the result of a super-imposition of new values, new beliefs, new attitudes on a hard core of traditional practices and beliefs. This dualism occurs in both urban and rural areas to varying degrees. And a powerful influence on all sectors of contemporary society is the reward system established for the modern sector. It is argued that while we may incorporate and adapt traditional practices in education we must ensure that the child from even apparently the most remote area has equal opportunity with the urban child to go to secondary school and eventually to University, because these are now conceived as the 'rewards' within the education system [133, p. 18].

The role of languages, and more particularly that of the mother tongue, has already been briefly mentioned (see p. 89). But we must return to it, as it involves a fundamental problem which is now confronting a large number of developing countries.

To start with, we have to point out that the question is much more complex than it appears at first glance. It has some purely educational implications, but at the same time certain cultural, social, economic and political aspects. Up to now, it has been solved in a number of very different ways. In June 1976, it was the subject of a symposium organized at Dakar by Unesco's Regional Office for Education in Africa, where all the important problems concerning education in the mother tongue were discussed. It is interesting to note that this subject is related to practically all the topics dealt with in this book.

At the educational level, it seems easy to support the view taken by a Nigerian educator, who writes:

> There is a consensus of informed opinion on the desirability of the mother tongue as a medium of instruction in the early years of primary school life. As the child's first language, the mother tongue is the means of verbal communication and it therefore helps the child in the process of learning and the teacher in instructing and teaching. In the early days at school, the child faces the problems of acquiring concepts and skills and of communication with the teacher and fellow pupils. The mother tongue offers some relief to the complex situation, so that the teacher and the learner may concentrate on the new knowledge which is being acquired. Communication in a foreign language would be difficult and it could mislead as to the nature of the child's difficulty [141, p. 34].

In many developing countries, however, instruction is not given in the mother tongue. Along with the education systems of the colonizers, these countries have inherited instruction in foreign languages. Philip Coombs notes that, in the African countries, '50 per cent of school time is devoted to learning to be literate in a "foreign" international language', particularly French and English [28, p. 89].

In the developing countries, one of the weakest points in education is the excessively high rate of school wastage. It has been proved that one of the causes of this problem is precisely the fact that the pupils are not taught in their mother tongue. The educational advantages of teaching in the mother tongue are also generally recognized in the case of adult literacy classes. Practically everywhere in the world today, adult functional literacy classes are conducted in the languages of the populations in question.

This question of languages is perhaps felt most acutely in Africa, a continent with an oral tradition. It is of concern to all African governments, as appears from the resolutions adopted by both the Intergovernmental Conference on Cultural Policies in Africa (Accra, 1975), and the Conference of Ministers of Education of African Member States (Lagos, 1976). This problem plays a central part in the many educational reforms and innovations which are being carried out in African countries. Even a hasty glance at the experiments in progress is enough to show this and to reveal the great variety of the solutions under consideration.

The United Republic of Tanzania, where Kiswahili has been used
as the language of primary education ever since there have been
schools in that country, hopes to become bilingual in Kiswahili and
in English. In a similar way, Malawi is using both the local languages
and English, while at the same time encouraging the introduction of
Chichawa and its use as the national language. Swahili is being used
more and more in Uganda, as well as in the United Republic of
Tanzania, and its recent adoption as the national language of Kenya
will undoubtedly bring about important changes in that country's
schools. In Madagascar, Burundi and Rwanda, primary education
is carried out in the national languages. In Zaire, literacy in the
Zairian language has been compulsory since 1974, and Senegal has
just opened experimental classes in the mother tongue (autumn 1976).
Somalia has recently introduced a Latin script and is deeply engrossed
in the massive exercise of changing the system, curricula and syllabi
over to the Somali language. Swaziland recently introduced Si Swati
as an optional subject and will progressively increase its use towards
the eventual goal of using it exclusively. In Zambia, an important
reform entitled 'Education for development', which provides for teaching in the seven national languages, is now being discussed. Other
countries, such as Congo and Upper Volta, are carrying out studies
in the search for solutions. However, there are also countries which
have deliberately opted for a 'foreign' language, as Ivory Coast has
done for French.[1]

However, it would be a mistake to think that this problem of
language exists only in Africa. In Singapore, for example, educational
policy is based on equal treatment, down to and including the secondary
level, of four languages: English, Chinese, Malay and Tamil.[2] Switzerland offers a similar example, for these problems are by no means
confined to the Third World alone.

On the political level, the problem is even more difficult,particularly
in a multilingual country like Belgium or a bilingual one like Canada.
It is unnecessary to point out the complications—even going beyond
the socio-educational field—which can be caused, in the former
country, by its division into eight types of area depending on their

1. This information is derived, first, from the Unesco/Unicef seminar report:
   Basic education in Eastern Africa [133, p. 19] and, secondly, from communications presented at the Dakar symposium on 'Education in the mother
   tongue'.
2. See: Ruth H. K. WONG, *Educational innovation in Singapore* [164].

linguistic majorities and minorities, or in the latter by the legal imposition of one language on the basis of a geographic criterion.

A genuine democratization of education will depend, to a large extent, on solving the problem of instruction in the mother tongue. Opportunities for access to education are especially unequal if the teaching is in a 'foreign' language, a perfect knowledge of which is the distinguishing mark of certain privileged classes. It is very significant that a country like Burundi has come out in favour of the 'Kirundization' [1] and ruralization of education in a two-part campaign. There are often linguistic barriers in these countries, in fact, between urban and rural populations which hamper rural development. Moreover, it is generally admitted that 'if national languages are used and promoted, this makes it possible for the population to be involved and to participate in development projects of an agricultural nature' [86a, p. 17].

Is it necessary to stress the importance of language in the search for cultural identity? Can an 'endogenous' and relevant education choose a foreign language as its principal vehicle? If the school is to be firmly rooted in its environment, if close relations are to be established between education and society, there must be a common language, in the literal sense of the term.

Up to now, we have only described the many arguments in favour of teaching in the mother tongue. But the problem is complicated by a certain number of difficulties and arguments. Some are of a technical or material nature, while another is, to begin with, the multitude of these languages, which in some African countries are numbered in the hundreds and which often have not yet been transcribed. There are no dictionaries, books, documents or textbooks, and no pedagogical methods have been worked out or teachers trained to teach in these languages. Still more serious are the social problems: the 'foreign' languages usually enjoy great prestige; they are considered a sign of culture and civilization, so that there is the danger that education in the vernacular may be branded as a cut-price education, especially in urban areas.

Moreover, it is a knowledge of one of the major international languages which opens the door to higher studies and to the coveted positions in administration, commerce and industry, as well as to political office. The language of the former colonizers is almost always

---

1. Kirundi is the national language of Burundi.

the language of the élite. 'Public opinion quite often regards the foreign language as the privileged and, in fact, only instrument for social advancement'.[1]

---

1. This is one of the conclusions reached at the Dakar Symposium on 'Education in the mother tongue'.

Chapter Five

Education tomorrow

Children who enter school today will be about thirty years old at the dawn of the next millenium and will therefore still be starting their professional careers. Those now being educated in school are the ones who will shape the beginning of the third millenium. The reforms and innovations conceived today will not enter into force until a few years from now and their effects will not be felt for several decades. Here is one example. 'The Swedish Riksdag passed legislation on a new system of teacher training in 1969. These teachers are expected to be active professionally for an average 35-45 years to come. They will be teaching young people whose own productive lives will run for about 50 years. This is by way of saying that the teacher-training decisions taken during the 1960s will have repercussions up to the mid-21st century'.[1]

By their very nature, every educational project and every measure taken in this field look to the future. To try to predict the possible futures of education is absolutely necessary as soon as an attempt is made to reform the existing education systems, i.e. as soon as any planning of education is undertaken. To plan means to make choices, to take out options on the future. But to plan also means to provide the necessary measures for carrying out a political intention. Any planning of education presupposes the existence of a political intention, for it is aimed at implementing a project of society.

A few years ago, the planning of education was still primarily thought of in quantitative terms. For example, it was a question of predicting the number of enrolments, at a given time, in the various educational establishments and the number of graduates who would

---

1. Torsten HUSÉN, 'The purposes of futurologic studies in education' [107, p. 35].

leave them, or of taking measures to ensure that the 'product' of education corresponded to manpower requirements, in the light of economic objectives, etc. 'The development of educational planning was dominated by the endeavour to establish quantitative relationships between economic growth, the manpower needs of the economy and the social demand for education by individuals and families'.[1]

To some extent, this type of quantitative educational planning has proved a failure. The principal reason is that manpower needs are not predictable in the long term. It is generally recognized today that educational planning should be integrated with a general policy of social development, which means that it should be part of a general planning of lifelong developments and innovations. Obviously, therefore, it should be just as much concerned about qualitative factors as about quantitative aspects,[2] for every policy is determined by systems of values.

To plan also means to map out a road for something towards a future which, although possible, can only be hoped for. To a large extent, the possible futures are determined by the present and by the past. The future is never completely open. 'There are several paths open to society at any point of time [but the] choices about the future are limited by the realities of the past' [107, p. 6]. The analysis of the problems to be solved and the search for possible futures [3] go hand in hand, and together they constitute the premises for any real planning.

The future of education depends more on external factors than on endogenous elements in education systems. The political, economic, social and cultural contexts will determine the education of tomorrow, as they do today. These contexts will vary from area to area and from country to country. However, just as we have already found a certain similarity between educational problems everywhere in the world, it can be expected that certain developments will also be similar. There are undoubtedly general trends or weighted trends which will influence the futures of education. Their respective influence obviously depends on more general developments. On economic growth, for example. Up to 1973, analyses of the future were unhesitatingly based on the

1. J.R. GASS, Director of CERI, in the preface to the OECD publication: *Alternative educational futures in the United States and in Europe* [107, p. 5].

2. Concerning this, see: Louis EMMERIJ, 'Alternative educational futures and educational policy-planning' [107, p. 9-30], and Torsten HUSÉN's preface to the report on the activity of the IIEP in 1975-76 presented at the nineteenth session of Unesco's General Conference, Nairobi, 1976.

3. The '*futuribles*' in the language of Bertrand DE JOUVENEL.

assumption of continuous economic growth. Today, such an assumption is, to say the least, highly doubtful. A slowing down of economic growth, if not a stagnation or even a prolonged recession, would very likely not only put a stop to the quantitative expansion of education but also to any renovations of the systems as a whole. We have already seen the first signs of this. There is a danger that the initial impetus of innovations may die down, especially in the industrialized countries.

If humanity, or at least a majority of countries, should enter upon a period of widespread instability and insecurity—which would seem to be the case—we would have to expect far-reaching changes in human relations. In their search for greater stability, social systems would very likely have a tendency to become more rigid. For education, that would mean a return to more authoritarian systems of teaching and, in a general way, a return to more rigid structures.

On the world political scene, we can perceive more and more clearly the crucial problem on which the future destiny of mankind primarily depends: this is what the subject of a new international economic order is all about. The task which we have to accomplish in the very near future is to find an acceptable balance between industrialized countries and developing countries, to create a solidarity of all human beings; this is absolutely necessary if the human species is to survive aboard this drifting, rudderless boat, lost in hostile waters, which is our planet. And this task is, in the broadest sense of the term, an educational one. The race has started between education and catastrophe.

A new world order cannot be exclusively an economic one. It will necessarily also be a social and cultural order [150]. In so far as it becomes—or does not become—a reality, it will determine the development of education throughout the world. Failure to achieve it would be a serious threat to world peace. On the other hand, if it becomes an actual fact—in other words if there is a real will to reduce the injustices of this world—the education systems of the developing countries would experience unprecedented growth.

However, even assuming the most optimistic hypotheses with regard to the resources which would be available to the developing countries following fully satisfactory negotiations about the establishment of a new economic order, it would seem impossible that those countries' educational problems can ever be solved by the traditional forms of academic teaching which were invented in Europe, mainly in the nineteenth century.

It seems very likely that the new forms of non-formal education which are being developed everywhere in the world will continue to gain in importance. Without going so far as to believe, like Ivan Illich, that the school as an institution is bound to disappear in the foreseeable future, it seems that education systems will undergo a certain 'deschooling' process (*déscolarisation*), which might be speeded up even more in the future. The teaching techniques which have been developed and which are continuing to come to the fore in the non-formal sector, and especially in adult education (for example, by the use of group dynamics) will have increasing repercussions on academic teaching. This is also true of the contribution of informal educational activities: above all, the growing impact of mass communication media on education.

Under these influences, the school will be forced to open its doors wider to the surrounding world. In this way education will become more flexible and more relevant. It will break out of the excessively rigid framework of the traditional school and become more closely associated with the so-called 'cultural development' activities. This flexibility will be reflected within the school, where, for example, age-classes will be increasingly replaced by groups organized on the basis of knowledge levels. But it will also have the result that large parts of education will take place outside the school, especially in other, different cultural institutions.

However, the extent of this deschooling will depend on the economic future we have discussed above. It will be accelerated in a situation of growth and slowed down during a period of recession, if only because of the need for new schools—or educational and cultural centres—in order to free education from the constraints imposed on it by the excessively rigid structures of contemporary education.

Even if the concept of lifelong education is still far from meeting with general understanding, and even if no education system has as yet translated it into actual fact, it seems certain that in the long run this concept is bound to change the face of education throughout the entire world. Wherever important educational reforms are carried out, they will be conceived with this concept in mind. This means that education systems will become more coherent, but also more complex and therefore more unwieldy. It also means that more and more individuals will be engaged in learning processes. Pre-school education will become universal, young people will remain longer in school, and there will be many more opportunities for adult education, including opportunities for the elderly. As a result, education, which today is our biggest industry—in the United States there are more than 50 million young people in school, and India now has more than 100 million schoolchildren—may come to absorb a growing percentage of national budgets. It will therefore be necessary to find cheaper and more efficient kinds of education than we have today.

The expansion of education systems will make them still more inert and more resistant to change than they already are. Far-reaching reforms will have to be backed up by particularly powerful forces if they are to succeed. There is a danger that the 'old democracies', where unstable political situations seem to be gradually arising, may lose the necessary strength to launch important reforms. Presumably, the most remarkable educational innovations in the future will appear in the 'young' developing countries.

In many countries, one of the priority objectives of educational policy is the democratization of education. This trend will continue and will probably be reinforced by growing decentralization, particularly in the administration of education systems. However, it is likely that lessons will be learned from certain failures in the field of equality of opportunity. It may be assumed that the idea of equality will be developed still further and in greater detail. This will be encouraged by the strong trends towards individualized instruction. Equality no longer means the 'same education for all', but the 'best education for everyone'.

The democratization of education will add still further to the pressure on education at the higher levels. There is a danger that the difficulties and tensions caused by this pressure—unemployment among university graduates, *numerus clausus*, etc.—will become more serious. The remedies for this situation will not be found in education systems. It may well be asked whether this problem could not be solved by a different division of labour.[1] It is also possible that we may be moving towards an increasingly strong meritocracy.

With regard to the democratization of education, there will probably continue to be a tendency to standardize teaching instruction up to the end of the first stage of secondary school, but adding an increasingly wide choice of options to this common core. And this also for another reason. The development of science and technology will continue to make professional qualifications obsolete more and more quickly. It will become the normal thing to change careers during a lifetime. The distinction between general and vocational education

---

1. See: Aldo VISALBERGHI, et al., *Education and division of labour* [157].

will gradually disappear, since the ability to adjust to change will become more important than the posession of specific knowledge or know-how.

A few years ago, everybody expected that in a short time education would be completely revolutionized by new educational technologies —from audio-visual techniques to using computers. There have indeed been some changes and innovations due to modern technologies. But much fewer than had been expected. Up to now, education systems have proved surprisingly resistant to the inroads of educational technology. It is therefore unlikely that any great changes can be expected from them in the future.

International and regional organizations are bound to play an increasingly important part in the future development of education systems. Several examples have shown us that the leading new ideas which guide the way to future national reforms are worked out in these organizations. It is thanks to these organizations that avant-garde thinking is crystallized and very rapidly disseminated. The international organizations are the great catalysts of thought, research and development in the service of all nations.

It is also the international organizations, and in the field of education Unesco first of all, which are creating networks for the exchange of information and experience—vital arteries which are really indispensable for modern processes of innovation—as well as structures for practical co-operation.

Nevertheless, there is a certain tendency towards regionalization in co-operation between nations. Regional bodies are tending, in some cases, to take the place of the truly international organizations, which have often become too unwieldy, too ambitious and also too open to political influences for them to provide, with maximum efficiency, the 'technical' services needed by governments. Perhaps the encouragement and co-ordination of regional activities will constitute new tasks for these international organizations, whose work in turn will also become more decentralized.

Growing interdependence throughout the whole world will also make international co-operation even more necessary in the field of education. As a result, the problems to be solved will be more and more similar and the exchange of information, the comparison of the solutions adopted and united action will continue to become more important. This co-operation will not actually become a reality unless it is based on a broad participation, not only by governments but also by the various groups of individuals concerned.

Bibliography

This bibliography contains only those books and documents which were necessary for the writing of this volume. National reports presented at the thirty-fifth session of the International Conference on Education provided the foundation from which the author worked, but these have been quoted rarely. All eighty-five of these reports have been reproduced on microfiche by the IBE, and a catalogue (*Bibliography: reports presented at the International Conference on Education, 1975* (IBEDATA: 77-1)) is available on request.

1. ALGERIA. Ministère des enseignements primaire et secondaire. Direction de l'organisation et de l'animation pédagogiques. *La réforme scolaire: objectifs de l'enseignement. Identification des contenus et des méthodes pédagogiques.* Alger, 1974. 72 p., illus., figs., tables.
2. ASIAN CENTRE OF EDUCATIONAL INNOVATION FOR DEVELOPMENT. *Inventory of educational innovations in Asia. EIA Nos. 1-56.* Bangkok, Asian Centre of Educational Innovation for Development, Unesco Regional Office for Education in Asia, 1975.
3. AYMAN, I. *Educational innovation in Iran.* Paris, Unesco, 1974. 35 p., bibl. (IBE experiments and innovations in education, no. 10) [Also published in French and Spanish]
4. BAMGBOSE, A., ed. *Mother tongue education: the West African experience.* London, Hodder & Stoughton; Paris, Unesco, 1976. 153 p., maps, tables. [Also published in French]
5. BECKER, H., et al. *Die Bildungsreform: eine Bilanz.* Stuttgart, Klett, 1976. 78 p.
6. BENGTSSON, J., et al. *Does education have a future? The political economy of social and educational inequalities in European society.* The Hague, Martinus Nijhoff, 1975. 134 p., bibl. (Plan Europe 2000. Project 1, vol. 10) [Also published in French by the Ministère de la culture française, Brussels, and in German by Kösel-Verlag, Munich]

7. BENNETT, N.; VORAPIPATANA, K. *Towards community-centred education for national harmony and development in Thailand.* Paris, Unesco: International Institute for Educational Planning, 1975. 27 p. (IIEP seminar paper, No. 13) [Also published in French]

8. BEZDANOV, S. *A community school in Yugoslavia.* Paris, Unesco: IBE, 1973. 40 p. (IBE experiments and innovations in education, no. 6) [Also published in French and Spanish]

9. BIZOT, Judithe. *Educational reform in Peru.* Paris, Unesco, 1975. 63 p., figs., map. (IBE experiments and innovations in education, no. 16) [Also published in French and Spanish]

10. BLAUG, M. *Education and the employment problem in developing countries.* Geneva, International Labour Office, 1973. 89 p., diagrs., fig., tables. [Also published in French]

11. BOUKLI, N., et al. *Mostaganem Institute of Agricultural Technology: an educational innovation.* Paris, Unesco, 1975. 46 p. (IBE experiments and innovations in education, no. 19) [Also published in French and Spanish]

12. BOWMAN, Mary Jean; ANDERSON, C.A. *Mass higher education: some perspectives from experience in the United States.* Working paper for the Conference on Future Structures of Post-Secondary Education, Paris 1973. Paris, Organisation for Economic Co-operation and Development, 1974. 145 p. [Also published in French]

13. CANADA. Council of Ministers of Education. [Background report on the state of education in Canada for the OECD review of educational policies] Toronto, 1975. 6 v.

14. CANADIAN EDUCATION ASSOCIATION. *Open-area schools: report of a CEA study.* Toronto, 1973. 40 p., illus.

15. CARTER, W.D. *Study abroad and educational development.* Paris, Unesco: International Institute for Educational Planning, 1973. 49 p., tables. (Fundamentals of educational planning, 19) [Also published in French]

16. COMMONWEALTH CONFERENCE ON EDUCATION IN RURAL AREAS, Accra, 1970. *Education in rural areas: report.* London, Commonwealth Secretariat, 1970. 314 p.

17. COMMONWEALTH EDUCATION CONFERENCE, 6th, Kingston, Jamaica, 1974. *Report.* London, Commonwealth Secretariat, 1975. 180 p.

18. COMMONWEALTH SECRETARIAT. *Education in developing countries of the Commonwealth: reports of research in education.* London, 1973. 310 p., tables. (Education in the Commonwealth, 6)

19. CONFERENCE OF MINISTERS OF ARAB STATES RESPONSIBLE FOR THE APPLICATION OF SCIENCE AND TECHNOLOGY TO DEVELOPMENT, Rabat 1976. *Statistics of scientific and technological manpower and expenditure for research and experimental development in Arab countries: analytical report.* Paris, Unesco, 1976. 31 p., tables. (SC-76/CASTARAB/1)

20. CONFERENCE OF MINISTERS OF EDUCATION AND THOSE RESPONSIBLE FOR THE PROMOTION OF SCIENCE AND TECHNOLOGY IN RELATION TO DEVELOPMENT IN LATIN AMERICA AND THE CARIBBEAN, Venezuela, 1971. *Development of education and science policies in Latin America and the Caribbean.* Paris, Unesco, 1971. 141 p., tables. (UNESCO/MINESLA/3) [Also published in French and Spanish]

21. CONFERENCE OF MINISTERS OF EDUCATION OF AFRICAN MEMBER STATES, Lagos, 1976. Working papers and final report. Paris, Unesco, 1976. [Also published in French]
  (a) *Education in Africa: evolution, reforms, prospects.* 63 p., diagr., tables. (ED.76/MINEDAF 3)
  (b) *Educational development in Africa: trends and projections until 1985.* 37 p., annexes. (ED.76/MINEDAF/REF. 1)
  (c) *Regional educational targets and achievements in Africa 1956-1972.* 36 p., diagrs., tables. (ED.76/MINEDAF/REF. 2)
  (d) *Report of exploratory missions to examine the proposal to establish a regional network concerning educational innovations in Africa.* 8 p. (ED.76/MINEDAF/REF. 3)
  (e) *Innovations in African education.* 57 p., map. (ED.76/MINEDAF/REF. 3)
  (f) *From Nairobi to Lagos.* 27 p. (ED.76/MINEDAF/REF. 5)
  (g) *Education in Africa since 1960: a statistical review.* 1 v., various pagings. (ED.76/MINEDAF/REF. 6)
  (h) *Wastage in primary education in Africa: statistical study/Les déperditions scolaires dans l'enseignement primaire en Afrique: étude statistique.* 123 p., diagrs., tables. (ED.76/MINEDAF/REF. 7)
  (i) *Manpower development implications of the new international economic order: a challenge to African education and training systems.* 6 p. (ED.76/MINEDAF/REF. 8)
  (k) *Final report.* 98 p. (ED/MD/41)
22. CONFERENCE ON FUTURE STRUCTURES OF POST-SECONDARY EDUCATION, Paris, 1973. *Policies for higher education: general report.* Paris, Organisation for Economic Co-operation and Development, 1974. 188 p., diagr., tables. [Also published in French]
23. ———. *Towards mass higher education: issues and dilemmas.* Paris, Organisation for Economic Co-operation and Development, 1974. 227 p., diagr., tables. [Also published in French]
24. CONFERENCE ON POLICIES FOR EDUCATIONAL GROWTH, Paris, 1970. *Educational policies for the 1970's—general report.* Paris, Organisation for Economic Co-operation and Development, 1971. 157 p. [Also published in French]
25. CONFERENCE ON THE DEVELOPMENT OF DEMOCRATIC INSTITUTIONS IN EUROPE, Strasbourg, 1976. *School systems and inequality of opportunity (Committee II, Subtheme I): report presented by Wolfgang Mitter.* Strasbourg, Council of Europe, 1976. 10 p. (AS/Conf/Dem 9-E) [Also published in French]
26. COOMBS, P.H. *The world educational crisis: a systems analysis.* New York, Oxford University Press, 1968. 241 p., bibl., diagrs., tables.
27. ———; AHMED, M. *Attacking rural poverty: how nonformal education can help.* A research report for the World Bank prepared by the International Council for Educational Development, edited by Barbara Baird Israel. Baltimore, Johns Hopkins University Press, 1974. 292 p., bibl., diagrs., figs., tables.
28. ———; PROSSER, R.C.; AHMED, M. *New paths to learning for rural children and youth.* Editor: Barbara Baird Israel. New York, International Council for Educational Development, 1973. 133 p., bibl., tables. (Nonformal education for rural development)
29. COSTER, W. DE. *The compensatory role of pre-school education for children from culturally deprived low income families.* Strasbourg, Council of Europe,

Council for Cultural Co-operation, Committee for General and Technical Education, 1975. 24 p., bibl. (CCC/EGT/75/24) [Also published in French]

30. COUNCIL OF EUROPE. Committee of Ministers. *Intergovernmental Work Programme: medium-term plan 1976-1980 of the Council of Europe.* Strasbourg, 1976. 59 p. (CM/76/113) [Also published in French]

31. ———. Council for Cultural Co-operation. *Permanent education: the basis and essentials.* Strasbourg, 1973. 64 p. [Also published in French]

32. ———. ———. *Permanent education, a framework for recurrent education: theory and practice.* Strasbourg, 1975. 30 p. [Also published in French]

33. ———. ———. Committee for Educational Research. *Problems in the evaluation of preschool education: report of a Working Party.* Strasbourg, Council of Europe, Documentation Centre for Education in Europe, 1975. 219 p., bibl., figs., tables. [Also published in French]

34. ———. ———. Committee for Out-of-School Education. *Permanent education: fundamentals for an integrated educational policy.* Strasbourg, 1971. 59 p. (Studies on permanent education, No. 21/1971) [Also published in French]

35. ———. ———. Committee for Out-of-School Education and Cultural Development, 6th session, Strasbourg, 1975. *The school in its relations with the community: Secretariat discussion paper.* Strasbourg, 1975. 8 p. (CCC/EES/DC/78/8 Rev.) [Also published in French]

36. ———. ———. Steering Group on Permanent Education. *Interim report on the evaluation of pilot experiments.* Strasbourg, 1974. 75 p. (CCC/EP/74/6 Revised) [Also published in French]

37. COVERDALE, G.M. *Planning education in relation to rural development.* Paris, Unesco: International Institute for Educational Planning, 1974. 37 p. (Fundamentals of educational planning, 21) [Also published in French]

38. CRAUSAZ, Roselyne. *Diversification of tertiary education.* Report of the Working Party set up under the auspices of the Committee for Higher Education and Research, presented by the Rapporteur. Strasbourg, Council of Europe, Council for Cultural Co-operation, 1974. 41 p. [Also published in French]

39. DAVE, R.H. *Lifelong education and school curriculum: interim findings of an exploratory study on school curriculum structures and teacher education in the perspective of lifelong education.* Hamburg, Unesco Institute for Education, 1973. 90 p., fig. (UIE monographs, 1) [Also published in French]

40. ———, ed. *Reflections on lifelong education and the school.* Hamburg, Unesco Institute for Education, 1975. 80 p., bibl., tables. (UIE monographs, 3)

41. ———; STIEMERLING, N. *Lifelong education and the school: abstracts and bibliography/L'éducation permanente et l'école: extraits et bibliographie.* Hamburg, Unesco Institute for Education, 1973. 154 p. (UIE monographs, 2)

42. DEUTSCHER BILDUNGSRAT. Bildungskommission. *Bericht '75: Entwicklungen im Bildungswesen.* Bonn, 1975. 510 p., figs.

43. ———. ———. *Bericht '75: Entwicklungen im Bildungswesen.* Kurzfassung: Daten, Veränderungen, Vorschläge. Stuttgart, Klett, 1975. 79 p., diagrs., fig., tables.

44. ———. ———. *Strukturplan für das Bildungswesen.* Stuttgart, Klett, 1973. 368 p. (Empfehlungen der Bildungskommission)

45. DUMONT, B. *Functional literacy in Mali: training for development.* Paris, Unesco, 1973. 67 p., illus., figs., map. (Educational studies and documents, No. 10) [Also published in French]

46. EDUCATIONAL DEVELOPMENT CONFERENCE, 1973-74. Working Party on Aims and Objectives. *Educational aims and objectives: report.* Wellington, 1974. 35 p.

47. EDUCATIONAL RESEARCH SYMPOSIUM ON RESEARCH INTO PRE-SCHOOL EDUCATION, Jyväskylä, Finland, 1971. *Research into pre-school education.* Strasbourg, Documentation Centre for Education in Europe, Council of Europe, 1972. 80 p., bibl.

48. EGGER, E.; BLANC, E. *Education in Switzerland.* Geneva, Swiss Educational Documentation Centre, 1974. 47 p., fig., table. [Also published in French]

49. EMMERIJ, L. Education and employment: some preliminary findings and thoughts. *International labour review* (Geneva, International Labour Office), vol. 107, no. 1, January 1973. p. 31-42. [Also published in French]

50. ERDOS, Renée F. *Establishing an institution teaching by correspondence.* Paris, Unesco, 1975. 59 p., bibl., figs. (IBE experiments and innovations in education, no. 17) [Also published in French and Spanish]

51. ——. *Teaching by correspondence.* London, Longmans, Green; Paris, Unesco, 1967. xvii, 218 p., illus., diagrs., tables. (Unesco source books on curricula and methods, 3) [Also published in French and Spanish]

52. ERICSSON, Britta. *Admission to tertiary education in Sweden: new qualification criteria and new principles for admission.* Report submitted to the 9th meeting of the Working Party on the Diversification of Tertiary Education, Stockholm, 1975. Strasbourg, Council of Europe, Council for Cultural Co-operation, Committee for Higher Education and Research, 1975. 6 p. (CCC/ESR/75/97) [Also published in French]

53. *The Experimental World Literacy Programme: a critical assessment* [by an Expert Group. Chairman: James Robbins Kidd]. Paris, Unesco, 1976. 198 p., bibl., tables. [Published jointly by Unesco and the United Nations Development Programme (UNDP). Also published in French]

54. FAURE, E. et al. *Learning to be: the world of education today and tomorrow.* Paris, Unesco; London, Harrap, 1972. 313 p., diagrs., tables. [Also published in French and Spanish]

55. FIGUEROA, M.; PRIETO, A.; GUTIÉRREZ, R. *The basic secondary school in the country: an educational innovation in Cuba.* Paris, Unesco, 1974. 47 p., tables. (IBE experiments and innovations in education, no. 7) [Also published in French and Spanish]

56. FRAGNIÈRE, G., ed. *Education without frontiers: a study of the future of education from the European Cultural Foundation's 'Plan Europe 2000'.* London, Duckworth, 1976. xiv, 207 p. [Also published in French]

57. FRESE, H.H. Permanent education—dream or nightmare? *Education and culture* (Strasbourg, Council of Europe), no. 19, Summer 1972, p. 9-13. [Also published in French]

58. FURTER, P. *Possibilities and limitations of functional literacy: the Iranian experiment.* Paris, Unesco, 1973. 59 p., bibl., diagrs., figs., illus., maps, tables. (Educational studies and documents, no. 9) [Also published in French]

59. GALTUNG, J.; BECK, C.; JAASTAD, J. *Educational growth and educational disparity.* Paris, Unesco, 1974. 42 p., illus. (Current surveys and research in statistics CSR-E-5) [Also published in French]

60. GÓMEZ DE SOUZA, L.A.; RIBEIRO, Lucía. *Youth participation in the development process: a case study in Panama.* Paris, Unesco, 1976. 101 p., table.

(IBE experiments and innovations in education, no. 18) [Also published in French and Spanish]

61. GRENHOLM, L.H. *Radio study group campaigns in the United Republic of Tanzania.* Paris, Unesco, 1975. 51 p., bibl., figs., map. (IBE experiments and innovations in education, no. 15) [Also published in French and Spanish]

62. HARTFIEL, G.; HOLM, K., ed. *Bildung und Erziehung in der Industriegesellschaft: pädagogische Soziologie in Problemübersichten und Forschungsberichten.* Opladen, Westdeutscher Verlag, 1973. 438 p., bibl. (UNI-Taschenbücher)

63. HASSENFORDER, J. *L'innovation dans l'enseignement.* Tournai, Casterman, 1972. 144 p., bibl. (Collection "E3", 24)

64. HAWES, H.W.R. *Lifelong education, schools and curricula in developing countries.* Report of an international seminar, Hamburg, 9-12 December 1974. Hamburg, Unesco Institute for Education, 1975. 146 p., bibl. (UIE monographs, 4) [Also published in French]

65. HOLMES, B. *Aims and theories in education: a framework for comparative analysis.* Meeting paper for the Panel of Consultants on Educational Goals and Theories, Geneva, 1975. (ED. 75/WS/30) [Also published in French]

66. HUBERMAN, A.M. *Some models of adult learning and adult change.* Strasbourg, Council of Europe, Council for Cultural Co-operation, Committee for Out-of-School Education, 1974. 76 p., bibl., diagrs., tables. (Studies on permanent education, no. 22/1974. DECS 3/DECS 6) [Also published in French]

67. ——. *Understanding change in education: an introduction.* Paris, Unesco: IBE, 1973. 99 p., bibl., figs. (Experiments and innovations in education, no. 4) [Also published in French, Spanish and Arabic)

68. HUSÉN, T. *Social influences on educational attainment: research perspectives on educational equality.* Paris, Organisation for Economic Co-operation and Development, Centre for Educational Research and Innovation, 1975. 189 p., bibl., tables. [Also published in French]

69. INDIA. Ministry of Education and Social Welfare. Directorate of Nonformal (Adult) Education. *Nonformal education for democratic rural reconstruction.* New Delhi, 1975. 24 p. (Question series, 2)

70. INDONESIA. Ministry of Education and Culture. Office of Educational Development. *Educational innovation in Indonesia.* Paris, Unesco, 1975. 50 p., bibl. (IBE experiments and innovations in education, no. 13) [Also published in French and Spanish]

71. INSTITUT D'ÉTUDES DU DÉVELOPPEMENT, Geneva. *Le savoir et le faire: relations interculturelles et développement.* Genève, 1975. 198 p., figs. (Cahiers de l'Institut d'études du développement)

72. INTERNATIONAL BANK FOR RECONSTRUCTION AND DEVELOPMENT. *Education.* Washington, D.C., 1974. 73 p., tables. (Sector working paper) [Also published in French]

73. INTERNATIONAL CONFERENCE ON EDUCATION, 35th session, Geneva, 1975. *Final report.* Paris, Unesco: IBE, 1975. 59 p. (ED/MD/38) [Also published in Arabic, French, Russian and Spanish]
    Working papers also published in French, Russian and Spanish:
    (a) *Main trends in education.* 21 p. (ED/BIE/CONFINTED.35/3)
    (b) *The changing role of the teacher and its influence on preparation for the profession and on in-service training.* 34 p. (ED/BIE/CONFINTED.35/4)

(c) *Projections of teacher requirements in 1985: a world and continental statistical analysis.* 23 p., annexes. (ED/BIE/CONFINTED.35/Ref.1)

(d) *A summary statistical review of education in the world 1960-1972.* 41 p. (ED/BIE/CONFINTED.35/Ref.2)

(e) *Note on the Unesco-ILO recommendation (1966) concerning the status of teachers.* 7 p. (ED/BIE/CONFINTED.35/Ref.3)

(f) *Teachers and other professionals in education: new profiles and new status.* 10 p. (ED/BIE/CONFINTED.35/Ref.4)

(g) *Strategies for the training of educators: how modern techniques and methods can help.* 8 p. (ED/BIE/CONFINTED.35/Ref.5)

(h) *The teacher's role and training: joint paper from the international teachers' organizations.* 18 p. (ED/BIE/CONFINTED.35/Ref.6)

(i) *Staff training and access to education.* 18 p. (ED/BIE/CONFINTED.35/Ref.7)

74. INTERNATIONAL CONFERENCES ON PUBLIC EDUCATION. *Recommendations 1934-1968.* Paris, Unesco; Geneva, IBE, 1970. 376 p. [Also published in French and Spanish]

75. JANKOVICH, J.L. *Requirements of European higher education for telecommunication facilities and satellite communication.* Final report. Strasbourg, Council of Europe, Council for Cultural Co-operation, 1971. 274 p., bibl., figs.

76. JANNE, H. *Pour une politique communautaire de l'éducation.* Luxembourg, Office des publications officielles des Communautés européennes, 1973. 61 p. (Bulletin des Communautés européennes, supplément 10/73) [Also published in German]

77. JENCKS, C., et al. *Inequality: a reassessment of the effect of family and schooling in America.* New York, Basic Books, 1972. 399 p., illus.

78. KINUNDA, M.J. *Experience in Tanzania in identifying and satisfying local needs in education.* Paris, Unesco: International Institute for Educational Planning, 1975. 26 p. (IIEP seminar paper, no. 14) [Also published in French]

79. LALLEZ, R. *An experiment in the ruralization of education: IPAR and the Cameroonian reform.* Paris, Unesco, 1974. 113 p., bibl., figs., tables. (IBE experiments and innovations in education, no. 8) [Also published in French and Spanish]

80. LEGALL, A., et al. *Present problems in the democratization of secondary and higher education.* Paris, Unesco, 1973. 238 p., diagrs., tables. [Also published in French]

81. LOWE, J. *The education of adults: a world perspective.* Paris, Unesco; Toronto, Ontario Institute for Studies in Education 1975. 229 p., bibl. [Also published in French]

82. McKINNON, K.R. *Realistic educational planning.* Paris, Unesco: International Institute for Educational Planning, 1973. 45 p. (Fundamentals of educational planning, 20) [Also published in French]

83. MALASSIS, L. *Agriculture and the development process: tentative guidelines for teaching.* Paris, Unesco, 1975. 284 p., bibl., diagrs., figs., tables. (Education and rural development, 1) [Also published in French]

84. ——. *The rural world: education and development.* London, Croom Helm; Paris, Unesco, 1976. 128 p., figs., tables. [Also published in French and Spanish]

85. MARTINOLI, G. *Triggering-off the process of self-management in permanent education.* Strasbourg, Council of Europe, Council for Cultural Co-operation, Committee for Out-of-School Education and Cultural Development, 1974. 8 p. (CCC/EES/74/35) [Also published in French]

86. MEETING OF SENIOR OFFICIALS OF THE MINISTRIES OF EDUCATION OF THE TWENTY-FIVE LEAST DEVELOPED COUNTRIES, Paris, 1975. Working papers and final report also published in French.
    (a) *Education and development in a new world order.* Paris, Unesco, 1975. 46 p. tables. (ED-75/CONF.604/COL.6)
    (b) *Final report.* Paris, Unesco, 1975. 30 p. (ED/MD/39)

87. MEETING ON THE IMPLEMENTATION OF THE RECOMMENDATIONS OF THE VENE-ZUELA CONFERENCE OF MINISTERS OF EDUCATION, Panama, 1976. *Final report.* Santiago de Chile, Unesco Regional Office for Education in Latin America and the Caribbean, 1976. 83 p. [Also published in Spanish]

88. ——. *General frame of reference for the discussion.* Santiago, Unesco Regional Office for Education in Latin America and the Carribbean, 1976. 49 p.

89. MIALARET, G. *World survey of pre-school education.* Paris, Unesco, 1976. 67 p., figs., tables. (Educational studies and documents, no. 19) [Also published in French and Spanish]

90. MOVIMENTO BRASILEIRO DE ALFABETIZACÃO. *5 anos MOBRAL.* Rio de Janeiro, 1975. 11 p.

91. NAIK, C. *Educational innovation in India.* Paris, Unesco, 1974. 50 p., bibl. (IBE experiments and innovations in education, no. 11) [Also published in French and Spanish]

92. NAJMAN, D. *Education in Africa, what next? An essay.* Aubenas, France, Deux Mille, 1972. 195 p., tables. [Also published in French]

93. ——. *L'enseignement supérieur, pour quoi faire?* Paris, Fayard, 1974. 188 p., bibl. (Le monde sans frontières)

94. NETHERLANDS. Ministry of Education and Science. *Contours of a future education system in the Netherlands: discussion memorandum.* The Hague, 1975. 261 p., diagrs., figs., tables. [Also published in Dutch]

95. ——. *Contours of a future education system in the Netherlands: summary of a discussion memorandum.* The Hague, 1975. 18 p. [Also published in French and German]

96. NIEHL, F. *Chancengleichheit ohne chance?* Stuttgart, Klett, 1975. 120 p., bibl.

97. O'FLOINN, T. *Report on the visit to the pilot experiment on guidance in Scottish secondary schools (18-21 November 1975).* Strasbourg, Council of Europe, Council for Cultural Co-operation, Steering Group on Permanent Education, 1976. 16 p. (CCC/EP/74/4) [Also published in French]

98. ONTARIO INSTITUTE FOR STUDIES IN EDUCATION. *Education on the move: extracts from background papers prepared for the report of the International Commission on the Development of Education.* Toronto, Ontario Institute for Studies in Education; Paris, Unesco, 1975. 307 p., diagr., tables. [Also published in French]

99. ORGANISATION FOR ECONOMIC CO-OPERATION AND DEVELOPMENT. *Development co-operation: efforts and policies of the members of the Development Assistance Committee. 1975 Review.* Report by M.J. Williams, Chairman. Paris, 1975. 261 p., diagrs., tables. [Also published in French]

100. ——. *Education in OECD developing countries: trends and perspectives.* Paris, 1974. 299 p., tables. [Also published in French]

101. ——. *Education, inequality and life chances/L'éducation, les inégalités et les chances dans la vie.* Paris, 1975. 2 v., bibl., diagrs., figs., tables. [Some text in French]

102. ——. *The educational situation in OECD countries: a review of trends and priority issues for policy.* Paris, 1974. 68 p., bibl., tables. [Also published in French]

103. ——. *New patterns of teacher education and tasks: general analysis.* Paris, 1974. 118 p., bibl. [Also published in French]

104. ——. *Participatory planning in education.* Paris, 1974. 390 p., diagrs., figs., tables. [Also published in French]

105. ——. *Reviews of national policies for education: educational development strategy in England and Wales.* Paris, 1975. 63 p. [Also published in French]

106. ——. *Reviews of national policies for education: Germany.* Paris, 1972. 151 p., diagrs., tables. [Also published in French]

107. ——. Centre for Educational Research and Innovation. *Alternative educational futures in the United States and in Europe: methods, issues and policy relevance.* Paris, 1972. 214 p., bibl., figs. [Also published in French]

108. ——. ——. *Case studies of educational innovation.* Paris, 1973. [Also published in French]
   (a) Vol. I   : *At the central level.* 616 p., diagrs., figs.
   (b) Vol. II : *At the regional level.* 443 p., figs.,
   (c) Vol. III: *At the school level.* 326 p., tables.
   (d) Vol. IV: *Strategies for innovation in education.* 296 p., bibl., figs., tables.

109. ——. ——. *Recurrent education: a strategy for lifelong learning.* Paris, 1973. 91 p. [Also published in French]

110. ——. ——. *Recurrent education: trends and issues.* Paris, 1975. 58 p., tables. [Also published in French]

111. ——. ——. *School and community: a report based on presentations made to a conference at Slaugham, United Kingdom, 15th-19th October, 1973.* Paris, 1975. 145 p., bibl. [Also published in French]

112. ——. Education Committee. *Policies for innovation and research and development in education:* draft statement by the Committee. Paris, 1973. 16 p. [Also published in French]

113. PANEL OF CONSULTANTS ON EDUCATIONAL GOALS AND THEORIES, Geneva, 1975. *Report.* Paris, Unesco, 1975. 10 p., annexes. (ED-75/WS/67) [Also published in French]

114. PARKYN, G.W. *Towards a conceptual model of life-long education.* Paris, Unesco, 1973. 54 p. (Educational studies and documents, no. 12) [Also published in French]

115. PECCEI, A. *La qualité humaine.* Paris, Stock, 1976. 352 p.

116. PHILLIPS, H.M. *Literacy and development.* Paris, Unesco, 1970. 55 p., tables. [Also published in French and Spanish]

117. ——. *Planning educational assistance for the Second Development Decade.* Paris, Unesco: International Institute for Educational Planning, 1973. 75 p., tables. (Fundamentals of educational planning, 18) [Also published in French]

118. PIERPONT GARDNER, D.; ZELAN, J. *A strategy for change in higher education: the extended university of the University of California/Stratégie de réforme de l'enseignement supérieur: l'université élargie de l'Université de Californie.* Paris, Organisation for Economic Co-operation and Development, Directorate for Scientific Affairs, Education Committee, 1974. 95 p.

119. *Prospects: quarterly review of education* (Paris, Unesco). [Also published in French and Spanish] Each issue contains a dossier:
    (a) Vol. II, No. 1/Spring 1972: *Architecture and educational space.*
    (b) Vol. II, No. 2/Summer 1972: *Reading today.*
    (c) Vol. II, No. 3/Autumn 1972: *Adult education.*
    (d) Vol. II, No. 4/Winter 1972: *Education and environment.*
    (e) Vol. III, No. 1/Spring 1973: *'Learning to be': the renovation of education.*
    (f) Vol. III, No. 2/Summer 1973: *Education for rural development.*
    (g) Vol. III, No. 3/Autumn 1973: *Secondary education, training and employment.*
    (h) Vol. III, No. 4/Winter 1973: *The European university in change.*
    (i) Vol. IV, No. 3/Autumn 1974: *The education of migrant workers— where do we stand?*
    (k) Vol. IV, No. 4/Winter 1974: *The practice of educational innovation.*
    (l) Vol. V, No. 1/1975: *Education in the least-developed countries.*
    (m)Vol. V, No. 2/1975: *The teacher in society.*
    (n) Vol. V, No. 3/1975: *Education and woman-kind.*
    (o) Vol. V, No. 4/1975: *Aspects of education in China.*
    (p) Vol. VI, No. 1/1976: *A turning point in literacy.*
    (q) Vol. VI, No. 2/1976: *Technicians for development.*

120. REGIONAL CONFERENCE OF MINISTERS OF EDUCATION AND THOSE RESPONSIBLE FOR ECONOMIC PLANNING IN ASIA, 3rd, Singapore, 1971. *Development of education in Asia.* Paris, Unesco, 1971. 164 p., figs., tables. (UNESCO/MINEDAS/3) [Also published in French]

121. ——. *Final report.* Paris, Unesco, 1971. 91 p. (ED/MD/20) [Also published in French]

122. REGIONAL EXPERTS MEETING ON FOLLOW-UP OF THE RECOMMENDATIONS OF THE THIRD REGIONAL CONFERENCE OF MINISTERS OF EDUCATION AND THOSE RESPONSIBLE FOR ECONOMIC PLANNING IN ASIA, Bangkok, 1974. *Final report.* Bangkok, Unesco Regional Office for Education in Asia, 1974. 35, vi p. [Also published in French]

123. REGIONAL SYMPOSIUM ON EQUALITY OF OPPORTUNITY AND TREATMENT IN EMPLOYMENT IN THE EUROPEAN REGION, Geneva, 1975. *Equality of opportunity and treatment in employment in the European region: problems and policies.* Report and documents of a regional symposium. Geneva, International Labour Office, 1975. 89 p. [Also published in French]

124. RENAUD, G. *Experimental period of the International Baccalaureate: objectives and results.* Paris, Unesco, 1974. 69 p., bibl., tables. (IBE experiments and innovations in education, no. 14) [Also published in French and Spanish]

125. REUCHLIN, M. *Individual orientation in education.* The Hague, Martinus Nijhoff, 1972. 75 p., bibl., tables. (Plan Europe 2000. Project 1, vol. 2) [Also published in French]

126. RICHMOND, P.E., ed. *New trends in integrated science teaching. Vol. II.* Paris, Unesco, 1973. 239 p., illus. [Also published in French and Spanish]

127. SABOLO, Y. Employment and unemployment, 1960-90. *International labour review* (Geneva, International Labour Office), vol. 112, No. 6, December 1975, p. 401-17. [Also published in French]

128. SCHIFFLERS, J. *Co-operative teaching and rural development in Africa south of the Sahara: an educational co-operative model.* Geneva, International Council of Voluntary Agencies, 1974. 60 p. (ICVA Document No. 17) [Also published in French]

129. SCHLEIMER, P. *A panorama of technical and vocational education in Europe 1962-75.* Strasbourg, Council of Europe, Council for Cultural Co-operation, Committee for General and Technical Education, 1975. 42 p. (CCC/EGT/75/19) [Also published in French]

130. SCHÜMER-STRUCKSBERG, Monica. *Preliminary report based upon member countries' replies to the questionnaire entitled "Links between pre-school and primary education".* Strasbourg, Council of Europe, Council for Cultural Co-operation, Committee for General and Technical Education, 1975. 20 p., tables. (DECS/EGT/75/91) [Also published in French]

131. SCHWARTZ, B. *Permanent education.* The Hague, Martinus Nijhoff, 1974. 246 p., fig., table. (Plan Europe 2000. Project 1, vol. 8) [Also published in French]

132. SCHWARTZ, B. *Revised analysis guide: notes to clarify the underlying assumptions*, by the Project Director. Strasbourg, Council of Europe, Council for Cultural Co-operation, Steering Group on Permanent Education, 1974. 34 p. (CCC/EP/74/7) [Also published in French]

133. SEMINAR ON BASIC EDUCATION, Nairobi, 1974. *Basic education in Eastern Africa: report on a seminar.* Nairobi, Unesco/Unicef Co-operation Programme, 1974. 175 p., bibl., annexes.

134. SEMINAR ON QUALITY IN THE EDUCATIONAL PROCESS: Education and Social and Economic Development in Africa, Lomé, Togo, 1975. [*Working paper*, prepared by Robert Mélet] Kisangani, Zaire, African Bureau of Educational Sciences, 1975. 25 p.

135. STANDING CONFERENCE OF EUROPEAN MINISTERS OF EDUCATION, 9th, Stockholm, 1975:

    (a) Organisation for Economic Co-operation and Development. Centre for Educational Research and Innovation. *Recurrent education: trends and issues.* Paris, 1975. 58 p., tables. (CME/IX/75/3)

    (b) Council of Europe. Council for Cultural Co-operation. *Permanent education, a framework for recurrent education: theory and practice.* Strasbourg, 1975. 30 p. (CME/IX/75/4)

    (c) *Country reports and statements from Iceland, Malta, the Netherlands, Sweden and the United Kingdom.* Strasbourg, 1975. 65 p. (CME/IX/75/5) [Also published in French]

    (d) *Progress report on international educational cooperation: Unesco, OECD, Council of Europe, European Communities, Nordic Council of Ministers.* Strasbourg, 1975. 79 p., addendum. (CME/IX/75/6) [Also published in French]

    (e) Ad hoc Conference on the Education of Migrants, Strasbourg, 1974. *Record of the proceedings ...* Strasbourg, Council of Europe, Documentation Centre for Education in Europe, 1975. 132, xi p. (CME/IX/75/7)

136. STOIKOV, V. *The economics of recurrent education and training.* Geneva, International Labour Office, 1975. 115 p., diagrs., tables. (World Employment Programme Study on Education and Employment) [Also published in French and Spanish]

137. SYMPOSIUM ON AGRICULTURAL EDUCATION, Newport, 1975. *Report.* Strasbourg, Council of Europe, Council for Cultural Co-operation, Committee for General and Technical Education, 1976. 42, vii p. (CCC/EGT/75/18) [Also published in French]

138. SYMPOSIUM ON PARTICIPATION IN EDUCATION AND TRAINING FOR PARTICIPATION, Brussels, 1973. *Report.* Strasbourg, Council of Europe, Council for Cultural Co-operation, Committee for General and Technical Education, 1974. 21, v. p. (CCC/EGT/74/24) [Also published in French]

139. SYMPOSIUM ON TEACHING INNOVATIONS IN SCHOOL SYSTEMS USING NEW METHODS AND MEDIA, Florence, 1974. *Report.* Strasbourg, Council of Europe, Council for Cultural Co-operation, Committee for General and Technical Education, 1974. 20, v p. (CCC/EGT/74/25) [Also published in French]

140. TA NGOC CHÂU; CAILLODS, Françoise. *Educational policy and its financial implications in Tanzania.* Paris, Unesco, 1975. 137 p., diagrs., tables. (International Institute for Educational Planning. Financing educational systems: country case studies, 4)

141. TAIWO, C.O. *The mother tongue as a means of promoting equal access to education in Nigeria.* Paris, Unesco, 1972. 47, 15 p., bibl., maps. (ED/WS/307) [Also published in French]

142. TECHNICAL WORKING GROUP MEETING ON THE MANAGEMENT OF EDUCATIONAL INNOVATION, New Delhi, 1975. *The management of educational innovation: report.* Bangkok, Asian Centre of Educational Innovation for Development, Unesco Regional Office for Education in Asia, 1975. 34 p., figs.

143. THOMAS, J. *World problems in education: a brief analytical survey.* Paris, Unesco, 1975. 166 p., bibl., diagr., tables. (IBE studies and surveys in comparative education) [Also published in French]

144. TRIPARTITE WORLD CONFERENCE ON EMPLOYMENT, INCOME DISTRIBUTION, SOCIAL PROGRESS AND INTERNATIONAL DIVISION OF LABOUR, Geneva, 1976. *Address by A.M.M'Bow, Director-General of Unesco.* Paris, Unesco, 1976. 5 p. (DG/76/15) [Also published in French]

145. ——. *Employment, growth and basic needs: a one-world problem.* Report of the Director General. Geneva, International Labour Office, 1976. 177 p. [Also published in French, Spanish, German and Russian]

146. TWUM BARIMA, K. *Education and development.* Accra, 1976.

147. UNESCO. *Case studies in special education: Cuba, Japan, Kenya, Sweden.* Paris, 1974. 195 p., figs., tables. [Also published in French and Spanish]

148. ——. *Education in a rural environment.* Paris, 1974. 64 p., bibl. (Education and rural development, 2) [Also published in French and Spanish]

149. ——. *Feasibility study of a regional system of tele-education for the countries of South America.* Vol. I and II. Paris, 1976. 160, 684 p., figs. (Serial No. FMR/COM/RCP/75/207-UNDP) [Published jointly by Unesco and the United Nations Development Programme)

150. ——. *Moving towards change: some thoughts on the new international economic order.* Paris, 1976. 137 p. [Also published in French and Spanish]

151. ——. *Technical and vocational teacher education and training.* Paris, 1973. 240 p., bibl., figs., tables. (Monographs on education VIII)

152. ——. *The training of functional literacy personnel: a practical guide. A method of training for development.* Paris, 1973. 104 p., figs., tables. [Also published in French and Spanish]

153. ——. *Women, education, equality: a decade of experiment.* Paris, 1975. 109 p. [Also published in French and Spanish]

154. ——. Department of Social Sciences. Methods and Analysis Division. *The Unesco educational simulation model (ESM).* Paris, 1974. 29 p. (Reports and papers in the social sciences, no. 29) [Also published in French]

155. ——. General Conference, 19th, Nairobi, 1976. *Medium-term plan (1977-1982).* Paris, 1977. 369 p. (19C/4) [Also published in French, Spanish and Russian]

156. ——. Regional Office for Education in Latin America and the Caribbean. *MOBRAL—the Brazilian adult literacy experiment.* Paris, Unesco, 1975. 70 p., bibl., figs., tables. (Educational studies and documents, no. 15) [Also published in French and Spanish]

157. VISALBERGHI, A., et al. *Education and division of labour: middle and long-term prospectives in European technical and vocational education.* The Hague, Martinus Nijhoff, 1973. 189 p., tables. (Plan Europe 2000. Project 1, vol. 4) [Also published in Italian]

158. WALL. W.D. *Constructive education for children.* London, Harrap; Paris, Unesco, 1975. 349 p., bibl. (IBE studies and surveys in comparative education)

159. WARD, F.C., ed. *Education and development reconsidered: the Bellagio Conference papers.* New York, Praeger, 1974. 328 p., bibl., figs., tables. (Praeger special studies in international economics and development)

160. WATSON, B. *The remedial role of pre-school education: mentally retarted children.* Strasbourg, Council of Europe, Council for Cultural Co-operation, Committee for General and Technical Education, 1975. 33 p., bibl., fig., tables. (CCC/EGT/75/28) [Also published in French]

161. WEDELL, E.G. *The place of education by correspondence in permanent education: a study of correspondence education in the Member States of the Council of Europe.* Strasbourg, Council of Europe, Council for Cultural Co-operation, 1970. 98 p., bibl. [Also published in French]

162. WOLFGART, H. *The compensatory role of pre-school education: children with a congenital or acquired defect in perception or motor control (multiple physical handicaps).* Strasbourg, Council of Europe, Council for Cultural Co-operation, Committee for General and Technical Education, 1976. 28 p., bibl. (CCC/EGT/76/8) [Also published in French]

163. WOLSK, D. *An experience-centred curriculum: exercises in perception, communication and action.* Paris, Unesco, 1975. 52 p., illus., figs. (Educational studies and documents, no. 17) [Also published in French and Spanish]

164. WONG, Ruth H.K. *Educational innovation in Singapore.* Paris, Unesco, 1974. 82 p., bibl., figs., tables. (IBE experiments and innovations in education, no. 9) [Also published in French and Spanish]

165. WORLD CONGRESS OF MINISTERS OF EDUCATION ON THE ERADICATION OF ILLITERACY, Tehran, 1965. *Inaugural speeches, messages, closing speeches.* Paris, Unesco, 1966. 91 p. (ED.65/D.31/A) [Also published in French and Spanish]

166. YUNG DUG LEE. *Educational innovation in the Republic of Korea.* Paris, Unesco, 1974. 43 p., bibl., figs., tables. (IBE experiments and innovations in education, no. 12) [Also published in French and Spanish]

PRINTED IN SWITZERLAND   [A.45] ED. 77/XXV. 8/A